USING

iPad® 2

Bud E. Smith

QUE®

Using iPad® 2

Copyright © 2012 by Pearson Education, Inc.

Library of Congress Cataloging-in-Publication Data is on file and available upon request.

Printed in the United States on America

First Printing: October 2011

Trademarks

All terms mentioned in this book that are known to be trademarks or service marks have been appropriately capitalized. Que Publishing cannot attest to the accuracy of this information. Use of a term in this book should not be regarded as affecting the validity of any trademark or service mark.

Warning and Disclaimer

Every effort has been made to make this book as complete and as accurate as possible, but no warranty or fitness is implied. The information provided is on an "as is" basis. The author and the publisher shall have neither liability nor responsibility to any person or entity with respect to any loss or damages arising from the information contained in this book.

Bulk Sales

Que Publishing offers excellent discounts on this book when ordered in quantity for bulk purchases or special sales. For more information, please contact

U.S. Corporate and Government Sales
1-800-382-3419
corpsales@pearsontechgroup.com
For sales outside of the U.S., please contact
International Sales
international@pearsoned.com

ISBN-10: 0-7897-4835-5
ISBN-13: 978-0-7897-4835-5

Editor-in-Chief
Greg Wiegand

Acquisitions Editor
Rick Kughen

Development Editor
Mark Reddin

Managing Editor
Kristy Hart

Senior Project Editor
Lori Lyons

Copy Editor
Apostrophe Editing Services

Senior Indexer
Cheryl Lenser

Proofreader
Language Logistics, LLC

Technical Editor
Christian A. Kenyeres

Publishing Coordinator
Cindy Teeters

Book Designer
Anna Stingley

Media Producer
Dan Scherf

Senior Compositor
Gloria Schurick

Contents at a Glance

Media Table of Contents

To register this product and gain access to the Free Web Edition and the audio and video files, go to quepublishing.com/using.

All media files are also available on the DVD that comes with printed versions of the book.

Table of Contents

About the Author

Bud E. Smith is one of the leading authors of technology books writing today. He has written more than 20 books about computer hardware, software, and the Internet with more than a million copies sold. Bud's recent books include *Teach Yourself Facebook for Business in 10 Minutes* and *Teach Yourself iPad in 10 Minutes*. He is also the author of the upcoming *Using Google Sketchup 8*.

Starting out as a technical writer and journalist, Bud then moved into marketing and product management for technology companies. He worked at Apple Computer as a senior product manager; at Google competitor AltaVista as a group product manager; and at GPS navigation company Navman as a global product manager.

Bud holds a BA in information systems management from the University of San Francisco and an MSc in information systems from the London School of Economics. He currently lives in the San Francisco Bay Area, participating in environmental causes when he's not working on one of his many technology-related projects.

Acknowledgments

I have several people to thank for their assistance with this book.

I'd like to thank Rick Kughen for connecting me with this exciting project; Lori Lyons for managing the editing process; and Chris Kenyeres and Mark Reddin for insightful comments in development. Apostrophe Editing Services and Language Logistics combined forces to straighten out my syntax, though any remaining mis-teaks remain my own. (Yes, folks, that one was on purpose.) Dan Scherf made sure that the trains ran on time in getting the media files onto the DVD and online.

We Want to Hear from You!

As the reader of this book, *you* are our most important critic and commentator. We value your opinion and want to know what we're doing right, what we could do better, what areas you'd like to see us publish in, and any other words of wisdom you're willing to pass our way.

As Editor-in-Chief for Que Publishing, I welcome your comments. You can email or write me directly to let me know what you did or didn't like about this book—as well as what we can do to make our books better.

Please note that I cannot help you with technical problems related to the topic of this book. We do have a User Services group, however, where I will forward specific technical questions related to the book.

When you write, please be sure to include this book's title and author as well as your name, email address, and phone number. I will carefully review your comments and share them with the author and editors who worked on the book.

Email: feedback@quepublishing.com

Mail: Greg Wiegand
      Editor-in-Chief
      Que Publishing
      800 East 96th Street
      Indianapolis, IN 46240 USA

Reader Services

Visit our website and register this book at quepublishing.com/register for convenient access to any updates, downloads, or errata that might be available for this book.

Introduction

The iPad is still new—the first product of its type, with no significant competition until about a year after it was introduced. Apple used the breathing room to ship its second version, the iPad 2, and it's been a huge hit. The iPad occupies a unique position: It's the easiest way to perform most computing tasks; it's the most flexible and powerful entertainment and education device available; and, it's a large-screen device that's almost as easy to carry around as a PDA or smartphone.

The iPad is a big success. Children and older people particularly love its ease of use; everyone in between likes how easy it is to carry and how fast it is to get started. Even today, try pulling out an iPad—either the original, thicker device, or the newer, thinner iPad 2—in a meeting or on a crowded subway carriage, and you may get asked by a friendly passerby if he can take a look at it.

The iPad is very powerful. Part of the reason is the access that the iPad has to most of the iPhone's built-in apps and the App Store, pioneered for the iPhone. The iPad can run almost any iPhone app, though only in a small version, or a coarse-looking doubled image. At the same time iPad-native apps, which look and work great on the iPad's larger screen, are widely available, and iPad users fill their home screens with folders full of them.

Getting Started with the iPad

People come to the iPad with all kinds of more or less relevant experience. In many ways, the iPad is just a big iPhone, though this is a case where size does indeed matter. So if you're an experienced iPhone user, you'll no doubt find using the iPad easy and natural. Some things you do with the iPad, though, may seem tricky, such as managing video files between your personal computer and your iPad, which is inviting for video playback but has limited storage compared to a computer. This book is full of tips and tricks for you, pointing out the telling differences between the two devices, especially iPad extras.

If you're a "power user" of some other type of smartphone, you'll already have a feel for most of the functionality possible on the iPad—except for the built-in phone functionality, of course. But you're likely to need help on the details to get fully productive, fast. This book is for you; just the facts, with a bit of humor.

If you're not a big iPhone or smartphone user, though, you'll find the iPad easy to use at first but potentially confusing when you try some of the more complicated tasks, such as finding and buying apps. This book may well save you a great deal of time, confusion, and hassle.

The iPad and the iPad 2

There have been two major releases of the iPad: the original device, called the iPad, and a newer device, called the iPad 2. However, Apple and most others only use the "iPad 2" name when they're speaking specifically about the fact that the device is new, or its new features; more often, both devices are simply called the iPad.

The iPad 2 is thinner, lighter, and faster. Versions that are 3G-enabled also support the U.S.-centric CDMA standard, and the worldwide GSM standard supported by the original iPad. None of those improvements, though, directly affect how you make it do things. In terms of using the iPad, there are only two real differences that you'll find with the newer iPad 2:

- **Front- and rear-facing cameras:** The cameras that adorn the iPad 2 support the use of Apple's FaceTime software to make video phone calls and enable you to take low-resolution pictures and capture low-resolution video clips.

- **Three-axis gyroscope:** The iPad 2 added a three-axis gyroscope—which is more accurate than the two-axis kind that some other devices have. The original iPad didn't have any gyroscope. The new gyroscope is useful only for navigation (it helps establish the direction in which you want to travel) and for specific programs that use orientation data, such as games.

Because the devices work so similarly, I refer to them both throughout this book as "the iPad." When specifically discussing the cameras, FaceTime, or the three-axis gyroscope, I'll make specific reference to the iPad 2 to emphasize that this is functionality not available on the original iPad.

Welcome to *USING iPad 2*

This book tells you how to wring a great deal of functionality out of an iPad, including highlights such as syncing multiple email accounts to your iPad; surfing the Web, enjoying the engaging experience, while working around the lack of Flash multimedia playback support; using the front- and rear-facing cameras for photos, video phone calls, and capturing movie clips (on the iPad 2 only); and managing movies, music, and other large files between your computer and the iPad's limited storage space.

In support of all this useful information, *USING iPad 2* offers you the following:

- Straightforward, specific language and easy-to-follow steps

- Instructions on using all the apps that come with the iPad so that you have complete understanding of the basics

- Techniques for customizing and configuring your iPad so your investment—for the iPad and for add-ons that you buy to go with it—is rewarding

- Explanations of key terms and concepts, taking you from new user to expert

- Real-world examples related to normal daily use of the iPad, plus insider's tips on taking your iPad use further

Because this book covers the original **iPad**, the **iPad 2**, and the iPad 2 with **iOS 5** installed, there are some minor differences between the figures shown in the book and the media included with the book. These differences are inconsequential to the operation of the iPad or the instructions I provide for using your iPad. One such inconsistency is that the music player on the iPad and iPad 2 is called "iPod." With the release of iOS 5, "iPod" now becomes "Music." Tapping this icon, regardless of whether it's called iPod or Music, does the same thing—it fires up the music player. These inconsistencies are minor and don't affect the instructions I provide here or in the media files.

Using This Book

This USING book enables you to create your own learning experience. The step-by-step instructions in the book give you a solid foundation for using the iPad, and the rich and varied online content, including video tutorials and audio sidebars, provide the following:

- Demonstrations of step-by-step tasks covered in the book

- Additional tips or information on a topic

- Practical advice and suggestions

- Directions for more advanced tasks not covered in detail in the book

Here's a quick look at a few structural features designed to help you get the most out of this book:

- **Chapter objective:** Each chapter begins with the objective addressed in that chapter.

- **Notes:** Notes provide additional commentary or explanation that doesn't fit neatly into the surrounding text. Notes give details on how something works, alternative ways to perform a task, and other tidbits.

- **Cross references:** Many topics are connected to other topics in various ways. Cross references help you link related information together, no matter where that information appears in the book. When another section is related to one you are reading, a cross reference directs you to another section in the book where you can find the related information.

 LET ME TRY IT   *Let Me Try It tasks are presented in a step-by-step sequence so you can easily follow along.*

 SHOW ME   *Show Me videos walk through tasks you've just got to see—including bonus advanced techniques.*

 TELL ME MORE   *Tell Me More audios deliver practical insights from the experts.*

Special Features

More than just a book, your USING product integrates step-by-step video tutorials and valuable audio sidebars delivered through the free Web Edition that comes with every USING book. For the price of the book, you get online access anywhere with a web connection—no books to carry, updated content as the technology changes, and the benefit of video and audio learning.

About the USING Web Edition

The Web Edition of every USING book is powered by **Safari Books Online**, enabling you to access the video tutorials and valuable audio sidebars. Plus you can search the contents of the book, highlight text and attach a note to that text, print your notes and highlights in a custom summary, and cut and paste directly from Safari Books Online.

To register this product and gain access to the **Free Web Edition** and the audio and video files, go to **quepublishing.com/using**.

About the DVD—for Print Books Only

Print versions of the book also include a DVD with the same step-by-step video tutorials and valuable audio sidebars that are available from the Free Web Edition.

This chapter introduces you to your iPad and takes you on a tour of its controls.

1

Getting to Know Your iPad

The original iPad is a thing of beauty, likely to be admired whenever you bring it out in the presence of people who haven't spent much time with one. The iPad 2 is even more attractive—thinner, lighter, and truly elegant. Both models of the iPad have deservedly earned praise from reviewers, users, and even competitors.

Part of the iPad's beauty is its sheer simplicity. It has few buttons or switches and few connecting ports to the outside world. Unlike personal computers, which bristle with buttons and connectors, the iPad is simplicity itself. Here, you see how to use the iPad's controls with grace and élan, matching the device.

Pressing the Home Button

The Home button, shown in Figure 1.1, is the round button with an icon of a round-cornered square on it. When you hold the iPad upright, in portrait mode (as shown in the figure), the Home button is located on the front of your iPad, near the bottom edge, in the center. It's the only physical control or connector that you can see when you look at the iPad straight on. While using your iPad, you'll return to the Home button again and again. It is, indeed, your home base for using your iPad.

What does the Home button do? Briefly, it wakes your iPad up; it takes you from an app or some other screen back to the first Home screen; and, if you double-press it, it shows you a list of recently used apps, from which you can jump to any of them.

Home button

Figure 1.1 *Press the Home button once to wake up your iPad or to return to the Home screen. Double-press it to see recently used apps.*

If your iPad is in standby mode, press the Home button—or tap the Power button, as described here—to wake it up. The iPad then displays the Unlock screen, as shown in Figure 1.2.

Your iPad uses little energy when in standby mode—only about 1% of what it uses when turned on. The iPad can wait on standby for about 30 days, according to Apple, before running out of power. (I've never tested this because I would need to not use my iPad for a month to be sure—and I don't want to go without it for that long.)

Press, hold, and
slide to the right

Figure 1.2   *Drag the slider all the way to the right to unlock your iPad.*

If your iPad is already on and awake, you can do different things by pressing the Home button either once or twice. Press the Home button once to return to the first page of the Home screen. The current screen slides away, and the Home screen appears in its place.

If you are already on the first page of the Home screen, press the Home button again to display the Search screen.

 For details about searching for data on your iPad, see "Searching the iPad" in Chapter 2.

Press the Home button twice to display a list of currently running apps.

There's a subtlety here. If you press the Home button twice in a row, quickly, that's a double-press, and you then see a list of currently running apps.

If, however, you press Home twice in a row but more slowly, that's two separate presses. You then see the first screen of the Home screen after the first button press and the Search screen after the second one. This shows the difference between a double-press and two separate presses in succession.

Using the Sleep/Wake Button

The Sleep/Wake button is the oval button at the upper right of the iPad when it's held upright in portrait mode (refer to Figure 1.1). The Sleep/Wake button works differently depending on whether the iPad is powered off, asleep, or running.

Sleep/Wake with the iPad Off

If the iPad has been powered off—not just put to sleep—you can only power it back on again with the Sleep/Wake button. Follow these steps to power up the iPad:

 LET ME TRY IT

Powering Up an iPad That's Turned Off

1. Press and hold down the Sleep/Wake button for about a full second.

   If you hold down the Sleep/Wake button too briefly, nothing happens. After a wait of about 10 seconds, the Unlock screen and the battery power indicator appear.

2. Drag the slider to the right within about 8 seconds.

   If you drag the slider to the right within the given amount of time, it completes the power-up process and is ready to use.
   If you do not, it goes to sleep.

The process for using the Sleep/Wake button or Home button to wake up the iPad when it's asleep, rather than powered off, is similar.

 SHOW ME   Media 1.1—Powering Up the iPad
Access this video file through your registered Web Edition at
my.safaribooksonline.com/9780132709590/media
or on the DVD for print books.

Sleep/Wake with the iPad Asleep

If the iPad is asleep, you can wake it up by pressing either the Home button, as described earlier in this chapter, or by briefly pressing the Sleep/Wake button.

Press the Home button or the Sleep/Wake button briefly. The Unlock screen appears. Drag the slider to the right within about 8 seconds to fully wake up your iPad. If you do not, it goes back to sleep.

When the iPad is asleep, you can power it off—without explicitly waking it up first—by holding down the Sleep/Wake button for a longer period, about 1 second. The Power Off screen appears. Drag the slider all the way to the right to complete powering down your iPad.

Sleep/Wake with the iPad Running

If the iPad is running, you can put it to sleep by briefly pressing the Sleep/Wake button. Wake up the iPad by briefly pressing the Home button or the Sleep/Wake button.

You can power the iPad off completely by pressing the Sleep/Wake button for a longer time, about 3 seconds. The Power Off screen appears. Drag the slider all the way to the right to power down your iPad.

 TELL ME MORE   Media 1.2—Understanding the Difference Between **Sleep Mode and Power Off Mode**
Access this audio recording through your registered Web Edition at
my.safaribooksonline.com/9780132709590/media
or on the DVD for print books.

If you decide to not power off your iPad, tap the Cancel button on the touchscreen or wait 30 seconds. The iPad returns to being fully on.

When you're ready to use your iPad, press and hold the Sleep/Wake button for several seconds. This is described in the "Sleep/Wake with the iPad Off" section earlier in this chapter.

Working with the Orientation/Mute Slider

The Orientation/Mute slider is a small slider on the top-right edge of the iPad. It can do either of two things:

- The slider can lock the screen orientation of the iPad into horizontal or vertical mode so that rotating the iPad no longer causes the screen orientation to change. This is the functionality from the original iPad and is now the default for all iPads.

- The slider can mute the iPad so that no sound comes out through either the iPad's speaker or, if headphones are plugged in, the headphones. You can make the slider function in this way—as a mute switch—by making a change in Settings, as described in Chapter 18, "Customizing Your iPad."

The up position is the "free" position for the Orientation/Mute slider. It allows the screen orientation to change as you move or rotate the iPad or, if you've changed the purpose of the slider, it allows sound to come out of your speakers. The down position is the "locked" position; it prevents the screen orientation from changing or, if used as a Mute slider, it makes the iPad speakers, or any headphones that are plugged in, silent.

In the default mode for the Orientation/Mute slider, it controls screen orientation. Use these techniques to change screen orientation:

- To lock the current orientation into place, flick the Orientation/Mute slider down. Sliding the slider down exposes a small orange dot on the switch. The iPad screen briefly displays a rotation icon with a slash through it, and a small version of the same icon appears in your notification bar in the upper right and remains there. Your iPad is now locked into portrait or landscape screen display.

- To allow the screen orientation to change flexibly as you move or rotate the iPad, flick the Orientation/Mute slider up. The small orange dot on the switch is no longer visible, and the iPad displays a rotation icon onscreen. Your iPad is now in normal (flexible) orientation mode.

If you change the purpose of the Orientation/Mute slider in Settings, as described in Chapter 17, it works as a mute switch. If you've configured it this way, use these techniques to switch between silent and nonsilent modes:

- To put the phone in silent mode, flick the Silent switch down. You see a small orange dot on the switch. The iPad screen displays a bell with a slash through it. Your iPad is now in silent mode.

- To resume playing sounds, flick the Silent switch up. The small orange dot on the switch is no longer visible, and the iPad displays a bell onscreen. Your iPad is now in normal sound mode.

On the original iPad, this same slider locked the orientation of the iPad screen so that the screen display didn't change when the device was rotated. That functionality was replaced when iOS 4.2 was introduced in late 2010 with the Silence functionality only. Since the release of the iPad 2 in February 2011 and the release of iOS 4.3, the slider can be used for either purpose. My own take, after trying it every different way is that using the slider as an orientation lock is convenient but adds a bit of confusion and complexity; it's easy to forget what to expect when you move or rotate the iPad, especially if you move it only a little bit. Using the same slider as a Mute control is simple and clear.

Operating the Volume Controls

The Volume controls are on the right side of the iPad, below the Orientation/Mute slider (refer to Figure 1.3). The top part of the rocker switch is Volume Up; press it to increase the volume. The bottom part of the rocker switch is Volume Down; press it to decrease the volume. Holding down the Volume Down part of the rocker switch quickly mutes the iPad, just like the Mute slider when it's configured that way.

As you change the volume, a Speaker icon displays onscreen briefly, with filled-in dashes representing the volume level.

The Volume control adjusts the volume of music and sounds such as alerts and sound effects.

Using the Headphone Connector, Microphone, and Speaker

The top panel of the iPad includes the headset jack, microphone, and the Wake/Sleep button.

Because the iPad is not designed to be a phone, it does not have any built-in apps that use a microphone. However, some third-party apps, such as Skype—which adds phone-type capability to the iPad—and some games do take sound in through the microphone.

You can connect a pair of headphones, with or without a microphone included, to the headset jack. If a microphone is included, it should work normally with apps that use microphone input, such as Skype.

I find using Skype with a headset, including a microphone, to be a convenient way to handle phone calls with the iPad, especially while travelling abroad (when roaming charges for my mobile phone can be expensive).

In addition to the headset connector, which serves as sound output when a headset is connected, the iPad has a dock connector and a speaker in the bottom panel.

The speaker serves as the iPad's sound output unless a headset is connected. It produces sound that is, perhaps, surprisingly good, given the speaker's small size and position on the bottom of the device.

The dock connector serves to charge the iPad and to synchronize it. Charging the iPad is covered in the next section; synchronizing it is covered in Chapter 2, "Learning iPad Basics."

Connecting and Charging Your iPad

Your iPad works quite independently of any other device, but you need to connect it to your computer for two purposes:

- **Synchronizing and streaming:** As you will see in Chapter 5, "Syncing Your iPad," you need to connect your iPad to your computer to set up your iPad and to transfer information between them. Transferring information can be optional; when your computer and your iPad are on the same wireless network, you can stream movies and audio files wirelessly from iTunes on your computer to your iPad without physically connecting the devices. If you want your media files to be available when you take your iPad away from the same wireless network your computer is on, though, you have to transfer them to your iPad.

- **Charging:** As described in this section, you can charge your iPad by connecting it to a power adapter or, in some cases, to a computer's USB port.

  ⊙ *You can connect your iPad to your computer to synchronize information using the iTunes program on your computer, as described in the section, "Synchronizing Your iPad and Your Computer," in Chapter 5.*

You can charge your iPad by plugging in the power adapter and cable that come in the iPad box and then connecting the cable to the iPad's dock connector. (Using the dock connector for synchronizing the iPad and your computer is covered in the next chapter.)

The iPad recharges from a fully depleted state in about three hours. You are likely to find that the iPad recharges to about the 80% level quite quickly, with the remaining part of the recharge process proceeding relatively slowly.

For optimal battery life, Apple recommends that you run your iPad battery completely down and then recharge it once a month. You may find it quite difficult to run the iPad battery completely down because it takes about 10 hours of continuous use.

The iPad can also recharge with an iPhone charger, even though they take different amounts of power. (Most chargers are "smart" and dynamically adjust output, within their limits, preventing different devices from being damaged.) However, it takes nearly twice as long to recharge the iPad from an iPhone adapter as from an iPad adapter. If you get them mixed up, the iPad adapter is the one labeled 10W USB Power Adapter.

The iPad charges even more slowly when connected to some USB ports. A MacBook Pro USB port can sense that an iPad is connected and roughly double its output, though the resulting process is still slower than with an iPhone charger, let alone an iPad charger. Many other USB ports, especially those for Windows-based personal computers, do not have this capability and charge the iPad slowly or even not at all.

If you don't have a USB port that can charge your iPad, you can charge it by connecting the USB cable to a power adapter or sync it by connecting the USB cable to a USB port, but not both at once. This is a pain but unavoidable.

The iPad has a large pair of batteries that are about as wide and tall as the device itself and make up about half its thickness. You cannot access these batteries to replace them without breaking the iPad's warranty and most likely, the iPad itself. You do not have the option, for instance, of buying extra batteries, charging them, and then swapping them in for the ones inside your iPad when your iPad is low on power.

In this chapter you learn some basic techniques for using your iPad, such as using the touchscreen, arranging apps on your Home screen, and searching your iPad.

2

Learning iPad Basics

To get the iPad to do what you need it to do, you need to repeat certain basic operations over and over again. These include making gestures on the touchscreen; navigating and modifying the contents of the Home screen; searching the iPad's contents; and cutting, copying, and pasting data. This chapter explains these basic operations so you can practice them and gain skill in using your iPad.

Engaging with the Touchscreen

The iPad makes tasks that had previously been done on a desktop or laptop computer available on a device that's much easier to operate. The secret is in the touchscreen. Alive and flexible, it services as both an input device and a display device for the iPad.

You might use your iPad right alongside a desktop or laptop computer. If so, don't be surprised if you reach up to touch your computer's screen—forgetting, momentarily, that the only large touchscreen in reach is likely to be the one on your iPad!

The touchscreen is the most obvious difference between the iPad and a laptop or desktop computer. (Early in your career using the iPad, you might find yourself reaching for a mouse sometimes as well.) The iPad touchscreen is an exciting innovation, miles away from the often-clumsy touchscreens that have been available in the past.

Using the experience gained from years of success with the iPhone, Apple makes the iPad's hardware and software work together smoothly. The result is that using the iPad usually feels good. It's satisfying and immediate—using the iPad is a much more personal experience than using a "personal" computer.

The two main aspects to using the touchscreen are gestures to control moving among apps and using the onscreen keyboard to enter text. This section covers navigating with the touchscreen; the next section describes using the onscreen keyboard.

After you are comfortable using the iPad, using gestures on the touchscreen and using the onscreen keyboard blend together fairly seamlessly. It's worth it, though, to study each in turn, to help you get the most out of the entire touchscreen experience.

Screen covers are available for the iPad—clear overlays that go right over the current screen. These screen covers protect the screen from the oil on your fingers, dirt, and scratches. However, the screen is actually designed to work well after contact with your fingertips, so make sure that you experience the same responsiveness with a screen cover as you do without one.

Gesturing on the Touchscreen

The iPhone and especially the iPad are famous for the library of gestures that you can use on the touchscreen.

Following is the essential vocabulary of gestures that everyone who uses an iPad should know for basic productivity:

- **Tap:** This is what it sounds like—quickly touching and then releasing a spot on the screen. (Don't drag your finger between touching and releasing, or the iPad might not register your gesture as a tap.) Use a tap to start an action, such as opening an app, choosing an option, starting text entry into a text box, and more.

- **Double-tap:** Two taps in succession. Use a double-tap in apps such as the photo and mapping apps to zoom in—and then when you double-tap again, to zoom out.

- **Drag (or slide):** To drag is to rest your finger on a spot, move your finger, and then release—a tap with a slide in the middle. Also the iPad uses a slider control for common functions such as waking up your computer. However, what you're doing is dragging, even though the iPad shows prompts such as Slide to Power Off. In this case simply drag the slider.

- **Tap and hold to drag:** Some stable interface elements, such as the built-in and added-on apps on the Home screen, begin to shimmy after you tap on them and hold the tap. You can then drag the element, such as with moving app icons around on the Home screen.

- **Flick:** A flick is a quick drag-and-release. Use a flick as a quick way to scroll through a long list; flick, and the list starts scrolling quickly without further input. When you touch the screen, the scrolling stops.

- **Spreading and pinching:** To spread, put two fingers, or your thumb and a finger together, onscreen, and then drag each finger away from the other. In many apps, this is a quick way to zoom out. To zoom in, put two splayed fingers on the screen, and then bring them together (pinch). Spreading and pinching is often an alternative to double-tapping for zooming out and in, with spreading and pinching giving you finer control.

- **Four- and five-finger gestures:** Use a five-finger pinch to return from an app to the Home Screen. Use four or five fingers to swipe up and unveil the multitasking bar and to swipe across between open apps.

Unfortunately, the availability of some of these gestures is not consistent across applications. One notorious example is that you can't drag from one day, week, or month to the next, let alone flick, in Apple's own Calendar app (see Chapter 9, "Tracking Appointments and Events"). Other apps have special gestures that are hard to find out about but potentially quite useful once you do—especially games. Look in the Help function of an app, if provided, for instructions.

You should try all the gestures you can think of with a new app to see what works. The better you master gestures, the faster and smoother you can interaction with your iPad. Consider taking some extra time to experiment when performing tasks such as moving apps around on the Home screen or using Google Maps to look around a neighborhood onscreen.

Some apps have their own gestures in addition to those described here. Always try to research a new app to find out if it has gestures of its own, such as triple-tapping or dragging with two fingers (in apps that treat two-finger dragging differently than the usual one-finger dragging). Finding out about new gestures specific to an app may require some combination of looking on the Web site associated with the app, reading help files for the app, or trial and error.

 SHOW ME   Media 2.1—Seeing Gestures in Action
Access this video file through your registered Web Edition at
my.safaribooksonline.com/9780132709590/media
or on the DVD for print books.

Navigating the Home Screens

The iPad's Home screen is actually five separate screens, plus a Search function, as shown in Figure 2.1.

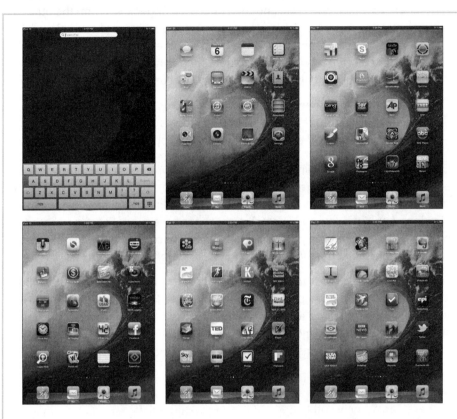

Figure 2.1   *The Home screen consists of one or more screens of apps, plus Search.*

The first screen of the Home screen, the one you see just after startup and after pressing the Home button, is the main Home screen.

To move around on the Home screen, simply flick left and right. You move from one screen to another; the little dots on the bottom of the screen update to show which of the screens you're on.

Specifically, flick like this:

- To see the next screen to the right, flick to the left—that is, quickly drag your finger from right to left, releasing at the end. When you reach the fifth screen of the overall Home screen, you can't go any farther. (You don't loop around back to the beginning of the screens.)

- To see the next screen to the left, flick to the right. You'll soon reach the main Home screen. If you flick once more, you get the Search screen.

- Press the Home button to return to the main Home screen from any other part of the Home screen or from within any app.

- To return to the Home screen from any app, do a five-fingered pinch.

Moving an App on the Home Screen

One somewhat tricky thing to learn how to do on the iPad is actually quite a basic function: Moving apps around on the Home screen to reorder them for future use. This might include moving apps to and from the Dock at the bottom of every screen, moving apps around on a given screen, moving apps into and out of folders, and moving an app or folder from one screen to another. (This last item can be particularly difficult.)

 For details about arranging apps and folders onscreen, see "Customizing the Home Screen" in Chapter 18, "Customizing Your iPad."

The following steps show how to move an app from the Home screen into the Dock at the bottom of the screen. The Dock has four apps in it when you get your iPad but can actually hold up to six apps. So if you haven't modified your Home screen much, you have room to move an app or two into the Dock, as shown in these steps:

 LET ME TRY IT

Moving an App into the Dock

1. Press the Home button on your iPad. The Home screen appears.

2. If the app you want to move is not on the first Home screen, swipe to move to the screen you want. If the app is in a folder, double-tap to open the folder.

3. Tap and hold the app icon. Release it when the icon shimmies.

   All icons on the iPad screen start to shimmy. A black X appears on the icon of any app that can be deleted, as shown in Figure 2.2. (Apps that ship with the iPad don't have the black X.)

Figure 2.2 *After you press and hold an app icon, they all start to shimmy.*

4. Drag the desired icon to the Dock.

   If there are fewer than six icons in the Dock, the Dock icons rearrange to accommodate the additional icon. If there are already six icons in the Dock, the additional icon can't be placed there—move an icon out of the Dock and try again.

5. To complete the change, tap the Home button.

   The icons stop shaking, and the X symbol disappears from the icons that were displaying it.

 SHOW ME   Media 2.2—Moving an App Icon
Access this video file through your registered Web Edition at
my.safaribooksonline.com/9780132709590/media
or on the DVD for print books.

Searching the iPad

A new iPad has little data on it, but over a short period time, the amount stored on it grows quickly. The ability to search the data on your iPad therefore becomes more valuable over time as well.

The data on your iPad can include contacts, calendars, notes, emails, bookmarks, and multimedia information such as music, photos, and videos. It's empowering to have it all available in a handy form on your iPad—and even more empowering if you can get to it when you need it.

Figure 2.3 shows the Search screen on your iPad in a close-up view. You can reach the Search screen by going to the Home screen (by pressing the Home button) and then dragging your finger across the screen to the right. (The Search screen appears as the leftmost of the Home screens shown in Figure 2.1.)

Figure 2.3   *Your iPad has a prominent Search screen.*

Unfortunately, the search capability on your iPad, called Spotlight, is somewhat limited. Only certain key fields in each app are searched. However, the content (body) of emails is included, whereas it had not been previously.

If you're used to the search capability in, say, Gmail, which lets you extract a key email by narrowing down the contents of several fields at one time, you may still feel that Spotlight is a bit of a let-down.

Following is a list of what you can search for—and some of the key things that you can't search for:

- **Contacts:** First names, last names, and company names. You cannot search within addresses, phone numbers, notes, and other fields.

- **Calendar:** Event titles, people invited, and locations. You cannot search within notes or descriptions.

- **Mail:** The To, From, and Subject fields of all emails, plus the message text.

- **Notes:** This refers to the Notes app on your iPad, not to notes fields in other apps. Unlike notes and content fields in other apps, you can search for the full text of notes.

- **iPod:** Names of songs, artists, and albums; titles of podcasts and audiobooks. Understandably, but sadly, you can't search for words that appear in song lyrics or spoken text.

- **Video:** Video titles. You can't search for text associated with the contents of a video, such as closed captioning subtitles.

- **Applications:** Application titles.

You can also search within an app. The apps listed here have the limitations described in the preceding list; however, a given app may provide other ways to do more specific or powerful searches.

If you use the iPad's Mail app to search your Gmail account, you can search only the To, From, and Subject fields. However, you can use Safari to access your Gmail account via the Gmail Web site and use the much more powerful search capabilities found there to search your Gmail.

Setting Up Spotlight Searches

You can control which of the apps is included in a Spotlight search by using the following steps.

 LET ME TRY IT

Changing How Spotlight Works

1. Press the Home button on your iPad.

   The Home screen appears.

2. Tap Settings > General > Spotlight Search.

   Your iPad displays a list of apps that Spotlight can search, as shown in Figure 2.4.

Figure 2.4   *Set up your Spotlight searches.*

3. To remove an app and its data from Spotlight searches, tap the app name to remove the check mark.

   The app is no longer included in searches.

4. To change the order in which apps are searched and results are listed, drag the Stack icon on the right up or down to move the associated app up or down in the list.

   I recommend that you put your favorite, most-used apps first.

   ⊙ *For more on entering text, see Chapter 4, "Entering and Editing Text."*

Searching with Spotlight

Using Spotlight is easy and fun. Among its other virtues, Spotlight lets you open the app and, if appropriate, the data item that you need directly from the search results.

Use the following steps to search your iPad using Spotlight.

 LET ME TRY IT

Performing a Spotlight Search

1. Press the Home button on your iPad.

   The Home screen appears.

2. Flick right or press the Home button again.

   Your iPad displays the Spotlight screen.

3. Tap in the Search iPad box and then type your search text. Tap the Search key.

   Spotlight displays a list of contacts, calendar items, emails, applications, and so on that match your search text, as shown in Figure 2.5.

Tap in the
results list to ———
open an item

Figure 2.5   *Put the Spotlight on your iPad's data.*

SHOW ME   Media 2.3—Using Spotlight to Search
Access this video file through your registered Web Edition at
my.safaribooksonline.com/9780132709590/media
or on the DVD for print books.

In this chapter you learn how to get connected to the Internet, whether via a Wi-Fi network, using a mobile hotspot, or with the built-in 3G connectivity that comes with some iPad models.

3

Connecting to the Internet

The iPad can do much more when it's connected to the Internet. Among the built-in apps you can use with the Internet are Mail, the Safari web browser, YouTube, the App Store (as well as many of the apps in it), and the iTunes Store.

All iPad models have the capability to connect to the Internet via a wireless hotspot. You may well have one in your home, and your place of work, cafes, libraries, airports, and other public areas are among the places likely to have a wireless hotspot available. Some hotspots are free to use; for others, you have to pay.

You might also be able to generate your own wireless hotspot from a cell phone. Many Android phones, such as the Motorola Droid series, can provide a wireless hot spot by repurposing the cell phone signal that they connect to for phone calls as well as data transfer. This capability is usually free with Android phones; there's a similar capability on newer iPhones, called Personal Hotspot, but you have to pay a monthly fee to use it. The monthly free from one provider is $20 a month.

You can also get a MiFi device—short for "my Wi-Fi"—that also connects to the cellular network to generate a portable hotspot. At this writing, the cost might be one or two hundred dollars, or the device could be free with a monthly subscription. Monthly subscriptions run in the area of $40 to $50 a month for unlimited data transfer. These portable wireless hotspots can support up to five connections at a time.

Finally, many iPad models have a built-in cellular network connection. These models are called iPad Wi-Fi+3G; models without 3G are referred to as Wi-Fi-only. (iPads with this option cost more than those without it—at this writing, the list prices are $130 more for the 3G models.)

The Wi-Fi-only models are the stronger sellers; anecdotal reports from early iPad 2 sales in the U.S. were that roughly three-fourths of sales were Wi-Fi-only models. The growing availability of "normal," fixed wireless hotspots, portable hotspots, and MiFi units might have something to do with that.

If you have a 3G iPad, you have to buy a data plan for the 3G capability to work. At this writing, in the United States, only AT&T and Verizon offer such a plan. (Other carriers sell the iPad, plus a MiFi device with a data plan of its own.) AT&T has slightly different versions of the iPad 2 to support its respective networks.

3G or Not 3G? That Is the Question

It's a bit agonizing to have to decide whether to get 3G capability for your iPad before you buy it. I'll go through the pluses and minuses here; you probably already have your iPad, but you may be a repeat buyer someday. Also, it's more than possible that friends or family members will ask you for a recommendation.

The popularity of the 3G models seems to have declined since the initial launch of the iPad through to today. It's not only the additional $130 or so for an iPad model that supports 3G; it's also the hassle and cost of a data plan, which can cost any-where from $15 a month up to $70 or so. Not only that, the plans are confusing; they're measured in megabytes of data transferred, and very few people can know in advance what their needs will be.

Despite the cost, many early adopters of the iPad bought the 3G option. This has apparently declined with time. Having been involved with the iPad from the begin-ning, it seems to me that the most important reasons for this change are

- **Widespread wireless:** People often find that they can get a wireless connec-tion in their home and office, and many other places as well. Occasionally there's a fee, but much Wi-Fi is free. The times when Wi-Fi is not available are generally few enough and brief enough to not be worth the extra cost.

- **Tethering:** Having a portable Wi-Fi hotspot in your smartphone is a new option since the iPad first launched. Android phones started getting tether-ing as a free option shortly after the launch of the iPad 1 in mid-2010; iPhone 4 users got the Personal Hotspot as a $20 a month option from AT&T begin-ning in March 2011.

- **Too many choices:** When the iPad Wi-Fi+3G launched, the only data option in the U.S. was unlimited data from AT&T for $25 a month. At this writing, you can go to AT&T or Verizon and get a data plan costing anywhere from $15 to $70 or so. (It's a bit amazing that Apple's carrier partners don't seem to "get" the benefit of simplicity that Apple demonstrates continually.) Who needs the hassle of choosing a vendor and a plan?

- **MiFi units:** A MiFi, shown in Figure 3.1, is a portable personal hotspot that isn't a smartphone. It costs $100 to $200 a month at this writing, or might come free with a data plan that costs perhaps $40 or $50 a month. MiFi units became more popular in 2010 partly because of the need on the part of iPad Wi-Fi-only users for connectivity.

Figure 3.1 *A MiFi helps make your Wi-Fi-only iPad fully portable.*

- **Instapaper and friends:** Instapaper is an app that enables you to sync saved Web pages to your iPad and then read them on the go without a live Internet connection. There are also tools for reading PDFs and tons of entertainment options that can be preloaded, including books, songs, TV shows, and movies.

There are still good reasons to get a 3G iPad for some people. If you spend a lot of time on the move, especially internationally, the flexibility of a 3G iPad is valuable. Tethering your iPad to your cell phone for more than a half hour or so runs down your cell phone battery noticeably; it's much better to run down the much more robust iPad batteries. Also a MiFi—fun as it is—is still an extra piece of hardware to hassle with.

The iPad has its GPS hardware in the same hardware module as its 3G radio, so only the 3G iPad has true GPS capability. The 3G iPad also has a GPS-assisted GPS from the cell phone network. (This works even if you don't have an active data plan.) Wi-Fi-only iPads do get a location fix from Wi-Fi base stations, but this can suddenly disappear in less populated areas, and it's less accurate.

If you use the iPad as a "go-to" tool for work and your job involves travel (even within your local area), the 3G option is great; same if you frequently want to use your iPad for navigation. Many other people will want the flexibility of having 3G built in, even if they might not ever turn it on. And the long-run cost isn't that bad because 3G options increase the resale value of your iPad.

I think, though, that the "burden of proof" has shifted. In the early days, I would have said to get a 3G unit unless you were pretty sure you wouldn't need it—for instance, if your iPad rarely leaves home. Now I'd say to get a Wi-Fi-only unit unless you're pretty sure that you'll use your iPad on the move fairly often and that tethering isn't an option for you.

Joining a Wi-Fi Network

As you take your iPad to different places, such as your home, office, or a library, you might have the opportunity to connect to the local wireless network. Most such networks require a key or password. You might be offered access with no key, be told the key for free, or be required to pay for service to use the network.

After you join a Wi-Fi network in a given location, your iPad remembers any password associated with the network and tries to reconnect to that same network whenever you are in range of it. If you have connected to several networks available from a given spot, your iPad tries to connect to the most recently used one first. Use the following steps to join a network for the first time or to disconnect from your current wireless network connection and join a different one.

Sometimes Wi-Fi networks are available and open for you to join at your location. This may be because ordinary users have purposefully or accidentally neglected to secure their networks; because someone wants to offer free Wi-Fi to customers or others; or because people want to steal data from people who sign onto their free Wi-Fi networks. Some of these thieves use tricks such as calling their networks "secure networks" or other tricky names. There are enough data thieves out there that you have to think carefully before logging onto an open Wi-Fi network that you're otherwise unfamiliar with.

Here are the steps to look for and, if possible, join a Wi-Fi network.

 **LET ME TRY IT**

Connecting to a Wi-Fi Network

1. From the Home screen, choose Settings. Choose Wi-Fi and use the onscreen switch to turn Wi-Fi on.

A list of available networks appears, as shown in Figure 3.2. Password-protected networks display a Lock icon; you can't join such a network unless you have the password. Networks that are not password-protected might require a fee to use. The network's signal strength is displayed via the Wi-Fi icon for that network; more bars mean a stronger connection.

Figure 3.2   *The iPad displays networks available at your location.*

2. Tap the name of a network that you want to use. If the network is hidden, tap Other, enter the name of the network, and select the type of security used (None, WEP, WPA, WPA2, WPA Enterprise, or WPA2 Enterprise).

    If the network is password-protected, a request for the password appears, as shown in Figure 3.3.

3. Enter a password if necessary. Then tap Join.

    Your iPad connects to the network.

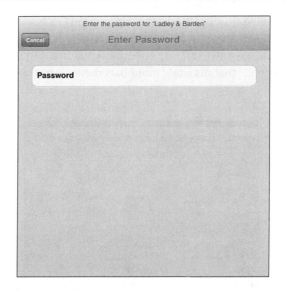

Figure 3.3   *Join the network you've chosen.*

4. If a screen appears requesting payment via credit card or other means, enter the requested details, or cancel and choose another network, or none.

The Wi-Fi icon displays in the status bar at the top of the screen. (If you have a 3G iPad, you'll see the Wi-Fi icon instead of the 3G one.) The strength of the network connection displays in the icon.

People use their iPads for phone calls using the Skype app, and wireless Bluetooth earphones are quite popular. However, pairing Bluetooth headsets and earphones to the iPad is officially unsupported and said to be hard to make work as well.

SHOW ME   Media 3.1—Choosing a Wireless Network
Access this video file through your registered Web Edition at
my.safaribooksonline.com/9780132709590/media
or on the DVD for print books.

Tethering Your iPad to a Mobile Hotspot

If you have a smartphone that supports the creation of a Wi-Fi hotspot, you can log onto your own personal Wi-Fi network using the previous steps. The specific steps for turning on a personal hotspot vary by the type of mobile phone you have, so I won't try to give the steps for that here.

Not only do you get 3G-type speeds with the ease of hooking up to a Wi-Fi network, but so far phones with GPS built in seem to pass their location information to the iPad that tethers to them. This means that a tethered Wi-Fi-only iPad has full GPS capability, just like a 3G iPad does.

There's really only one problem I've experienced with tethering: running the Wi-Fi hotspot burns through your phone's battery very quickly. If you have GPS turned on in your smartphone—so you can navigate using your smartphone and/or iPad—it's even worse.

My Android phone goes through batteries really fast; I carry an extra battery or two if I'm going to be out more than a few hours. (Like the iPad, the iPhone line-up has sealed batteries, but there's a strong after-market trade in add-on battery packs of various kinds.)

This is much less of a problem for the iPad. Using the 3G capability is estimated by Apple—and verified by others—to cut battery life from about 10 hours to about 9. This is not fun when it becomes a problem, but it's better than dealing with a smartphone battery life that seems to diminish by the minute after the first hour or two.

The data standard for fast data access over cellular networks is called 4G, and the first 4G mobile phones were beginning to appear just as the iPad 2 rolled out. The technology was still immature enough, though, that Apple seems to have been wise to use 3G, not 4G, as the cellular network option for the iPad 2. However, if you do get a 3G unit, you're stuck with 3G until you get a new iPad. If you tether your iPad to your smartphone instead for connectivity, you'll get 4G capability as soon as you get a 4G phone.

Joining a 3G Network

If you have a 3G iPad, it can automatically connect to the cellular network for which you have a data plan whenever possible. However, if you're not on the move, it's actually preferable to connect via Wi-Fi if possible. A Wi-Fi connection is more s table, more reliable, and uses less power than a 3G connection. Follow the steps in the section at the beginning of this chapter to join a Wi-Fi network if one is available in your location.

The 3G network used by the iPad is actually overlaid on two other kinds of networks: an EDGE network, or 2G network, which is a slower kind of data connection; and an analog cellular network, which is used for phone calls. Your iPad needs either a 3G or an EDGE connection to transmit and receive data.

The strength of the analog cellular network connection is shown by the well-known symbol of bars in the status bar at the top of your iPad's screen. These bars are not directly relevant to you as an iPad user, but usually more bars indicate a higher likelihood of a data connection.

The connection can sometimes be the fastest kind, 3G; other times, it will be the slower EDGE network. You can also be in a location in which you get an analog c ellular network connection—which the iPad can't use—but no data connection, neither EDGE nor 3G. In these cases, look for a Wi-Fi connection. In fact, you might want to look for a Wi-Fi connection wherever possible—it's likely to be faster and more stable than any kind of cellular network connection. Wi-Fi also uses less power than the cellular hardware in your iPad.

You can also be in a location that is theoretically served by 3G and/or EDGE, but in which geographic features, signal reflections from buildings, and even the weather conspire to prevent a connection. Data connections can also become overcrowded, preventing you from getting a connection one moment, yet enabling you to connect the next.

Unfortunately, if your data connection is unavailable or unreliable, your only alternative for getting a connection is Wi-Fi.

 TELL ME MORE   Media 3.2—3G versus Wi-Fi
Access this audio recording through your registered Web Edition at
my.safaribooksonline.com/9780132709590/media
or on the DVD for print books.

This chapter shows how to use the onscreen keyboards, which include alphabetic keys, numbers, and many special characters, and how to enter and edit text.

4

Entering and Editing Text

One "key" secret to the iPad's success—sorry about the pun—may be its successful use of an onscreen keyboard as a practical alternative to a physical keyboard. The relatively large size of the iPad screen, compared to smartphone screens, provides the sheer screen real estate necessary for an onscreen keyboard that can largely replace a physical keyboard. Careful engineering by Apple helps bridge the remaining gap.

It's common for new iPad users to buy a physical keyboard as part of their purchase, for the sake of productivity—then find that they rarely use it. Like the iPad itself, the onscreen keyboard is so convenient, while being "good enough" to get the job done, that it replaces a conventional solution.

Complementing the iPad's breakthrough success with onscreen keyboards, the device also provides other features to help enter and edit text. Placing the cursor within text and selecting start and end points for cut, copy, and paste are among the operations that the iPad makes practical, if not always easy.

In this chapter you can learn in some depth about how to get text into your iPad. As people increasingly use their iPads as an alternative to carrying around a laptop, onscreen keyboarding and text editing skills might make the difference for you in getting the most out of your iPad.

Typing on the Onscreen Keyboard

People who use or comment on the iPad often have a hard time describing the difference between an iPad, and how they use it, versus a laptop or desktop computer. The biggest difference between the two is in text input, because the most often-used method for entering text is via the iPad's onscreen keyboard.

It's easy to use an external keyboard with the iPad, and the cursor keys on an external keyboard can replace some of the functionality of a mouse. However, just about all iPad users use the onscreen keyboard at least some of the time, and most use the onscreen keyboard most or all of the time.

Using the onscreen keyboard, you're likely to find that data entry is roughly half as fast on an iPad as on a computer. You may find that you pick and choose which tasks you complete on each device so as to avoid doing heavy data entry on the iPad.

You can optimize your ability to enter text on the iPad in two ways. The first is by using an external keyboard, as mentioned in the cross reference. The other way is by getting good at using the touchscreen. Use the information in this section to get a feel for the onscreen keyboard, and then practice, practice, practice.

Typing Basics

The iPad's onscreen keyboard is easy to use and effective. Whereas there have been complaints about onscreen keyboards in the past—"typing on glass" is still not as fast or efficient as using a physical keyboard—the iPad onscreen keyboards are about as good as it gets. The relatively large size of the iPad's screen (compared to, say, the iPhone) and Apple's clever engineering make using the iPad onscreen keyboard quite easy.

To use the keyboard, tap in any area onscreen that requires text or numeric input. The keyboard appears, as shown in Figure 4.1.

Figure 4.1   *The onscreen keyboard "morphs" to fit your needs.*

To enter characters, simply tap the appropriate keys. Following are some highlights of text entry:

- **Single capital letters:** To enter a single capital letter, tap the Shift key once and then tap a letter.

- **Shift Lock:** You have to turn this on to use it, as described in the next section, "Activating and Using Caps Lock."

- **Automatic end of sentence:** To end a sentence, tap the spacebar twice. The iPad adds a period to the end of the last word you typed, inserts a space, and then makes the next letter a capital letter.

- **Digits and special characters:** The digits 0[nd]9 and a host of special characters are available by tapping the .?123 key (when on the alphabetic keyboard) or the #+= key (when on the numeric keyboard). See the next section for details.

- **Additional characters and variations:** To see variations on keys, such as an accented "e" or a "u" with an umlaut, or an upside-down question mark or exclamation point as used in Spanish, tap and hold a key. Variations appear, as shown in Figure 4.2.

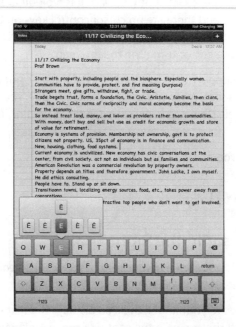

Figure 4.2 *Individual keys on the onscreen keyboard are packed with variations and related special characters.*

- **Typamatic Backspace key:** The Backspace key is what used to be called typamatic, back in the days of electric typewriters. That is, if you hold it down, it keeps going, faster and faster. When you hold down the Backspace key, it first deletes single characters; then, after about 25 characters, it switches to deleting entire words, at the rate of a few words per second.

- **Use international keyboards:** Add or remove international keyboards by choosing Settings > General > Keyboard. (That's the Settings app, General area, Keyboard option.) If additional keyboards are available when you type, you can access them by tapping the Next Keyboard key.

- **Hiding the keyboard:** Tap the Hide Keyboard key in the lower-right corner of all keyboards to hide the keyboard. Tap anywhere onscreen where you can enter text to bring the onscreen keyboard back.

> The onscreen keyboard is automatically disabled when you connect an external keyboard using Bluetooth.

Positioning the Cursor

Getting the cursor to the exact spot you want it is a bit different on the iPad. There's no mouse, of course, and there are no cursor control keys on the onscreen keyboard. (Apple's Bluetooth keyboard for iPad, like most other such keyboards, has one.) You position the cursor using the touchscreen.

The iPad provides support to help you do this accurately, but using it properly requires a bit of practice. After you master the technique, you can use it when selecting text as well. Doing so is described in the "Selecting Text" section, later in this chapter.

These steps show you how to position the cursor.

 LET ME TRY IT

Putting the Cursor in the Right Spot

1. Press and hold your finger near the spot you want to edit, on the same horizontal line.

   In the area above your finger, the iPad displays the text inside a magnifying glass, with the cursor in the center of the magnifying glass.

2. Slide your finger horizontally on the line of text to put the cursor right where you need it.

Verify the location of the cursor by watching the center of the magnifying glass, rather than your finger.

3. When the cursor is in the right spot, lift your finger.

   Don't drag or roll your finger as you lift it, or the cursor ends up one character off the desired location—an all too common result of this process.

Activating and Using Caps Lock

Some things in life are simply a mystery, and one of them is why iOS—the operating system shared between the iPhone and the iPad—requires users to turn on the caps lock capability in Settings before it can be used. I suppose it makes some kind of sense to turn it off, if needed, but making the "off" setting the default seems strange.

Oh well, it's quicker to fix it than to talk about it. Follow these steps.

 LET ME TRY IT

Turn On Caps Lock and Use It

1. On the Home screen, tap Settings. The Settings app appears.

2. Tap General. The General screen appears.

3. Tap Keyboard. The Keyboard screen opens.

4. Drag the Enable Caps Lock switch to On. The iPad enables the Caps Lock capability.

5. To use Caps Lock, double-tap the Shift key, or tap both Shift keys at once.

   The Caps Lock keys on the onscreen keyboard both display a blue background, showing you that Caps Lock is on.

6. To turn Caps Lock off, tap either Shift key.

Using the iPad's Five Main Keyboards

The iPad onscreen keyboard has some tricks hidden up its sleeve. The configuration of the keyboard can change at the tap of a key or when you turn the iPad enough to change its orientation.

For instance, when you need to type in a URL, the onscreen keyboard changes so that the spacebar is removed. Instead of a spacebar, you see a period key, a slash key, and a key that reads .com. Because Web addresses don't use spaces, Apple removed the spacebar and inserted keys that make sense when entering a URL.

There are actually five different versions of the keyboard that you frequently see when using the iPad. In addition to the main text entry keyboard, as shown in Figure 4.2, there are four others.

The first is the URL keyboard. This comes up when using the Safari browser app, with the entry point in the URL area. The URL keyboard is like the alphabetic keyboard, but with period, slash, and .com keys instead of the spacebar.

If you enter a word into the address bar, Safari adds www. to the beginning and .com to the end and makes it into a URL. For instance, to go to the Pearson Web page, just enter "pearson" in the address bar; Safari brings up www.pearson.com.

The second alternative is the numeric keyboard (with special characters), as shown in Figure 4.3. To access this keyboard, tap the .?123 key on the alphabetic or URL keyboard.

The special characters are

- / : ; ( ) $ & @ . , ? ! ′ 0

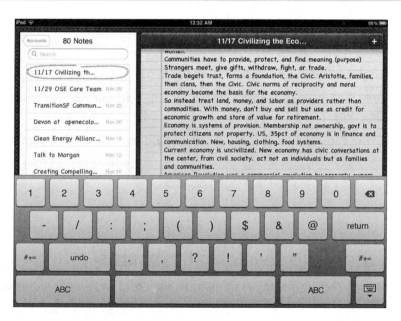

Figure 4.3 *The numeric keyboard includes the digits 0[nd]9 and 15 special characters.*

The third alternative is the special characters keyboard, as shown in Figure 4.4. To access this keyboard, tap the `#+=` key on the numeric keyboard.

The following special characters appear:

[ ] { } # % ^ * + = _ \ | ~ < > € £ ¥ . , ? ! ′ 0

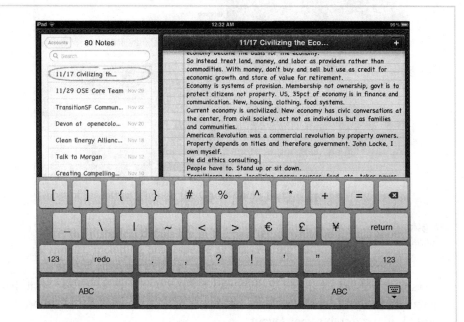

Figure 4.4 *The special characters keyboard includes 25 special characters.*

Note that the last six characters—the bottom row of the three rows of characters— are the same on both the numeric keyboard and the special characters keyboard.

The combination of different keyboards and additional characters available by holding down many keys makes the iPad keyboard much "larger," in terms of the characters supported, than any commonly used physical keyboard. The capability to switch the language used by the keyboards, changing the layout, adds even more power and flexibility.

The final alternative is the split keyboard, shown in Figure 4.5. The split keyboard was introduced in Fall 2011. It's actually two miniature half-keyboards, which together take up much less screen space than the full keyboard. The split keyboard is great for use with your thumbs.

Figure 4.5   *The split keyboard is a whole new approach to typing, especially if you're all thumbs.*

The split keyboard also has its own versions of the URL, numeric, and special characters keyboards. These have the same keys as the full versions described previously, but in the split-screen layout.

I personally found the keys on the split-screen keyboard just a little too small for my thumbs. When first trying the feature, I had the idea that you could resize the split-screen keyboard to fit your needs; but I sadly found that isn't the case. While practice makes perfect, you may need to be more dexterous than me to make good use of the split-screen keyboard.

Working with Predictive Text

When you type with the iPad, its onboard dictionary "watches" as you type and suggests a word based on the first characters you enter. As you type more characters, the suggested word is likely to change. When you tap the spacebar or a punctuation mark, or tap Return, the suggested word appears—*not* the characters you typed, unless they're the same.

This functionality is both powerful and maddening. Many of your typing mistakes are automatically fixed by the iPad, to the extent that you can allow yourself to be somewhat sloppy in your typing. In many cases, you can skip entering an apostrophe, for instance. (But in other cases, you do have to enter it, which can get confusing.)

However, many unusual words that you want to enter aren't recognized. For instance, starting to type the word "Smithsonian" generates the suggested alternative "Smithsonite." This seems harmless enough when the iPad enables you to complete the word you want and use it.

It's quite frustrating, though, when the iPad replaces the word you want to type with the word it thinks you want to use. (It almost seems like it's putting in the word it thinks you *should* use.) For instance, a popular slang term for "very" is the word "hella," especially in and around Oakland, California. "I hella heart that" means "I like that very much."

However, if you try to type that you "hella heart" something on your iPad, the iPad Dictionary changes "hella" to "hellas" ("Hellas", with a capital "H", is the word for "Greece" in Greek). To enter "hella," you have to explicitly reject the Dictionary's choice, or it will make the change for you.

Follow these steps to use—or ignore—the Dictionary.

> The Personal Dictionary allows you to add custom words and shortcuts to your iPad, for use in all applications. For instance, you can enter "Parslie", the name of a restaurant, so that it won't be auto-corrected to "parsley". You can also enter "prs" as a shortcut for "Parslie" – or for "parsley", or anything else you like. See Chapter 18 for details.

 LET ME TRY IT

Working with the Dictionary

1. Start typing a word on the iPad screen.

   In many cases, a word suggested by the Dictionary appears underneath the word you're typing, as shown in Figure 4.6.

2. To accept the suggested word, type a space, punctuation mark such as a comma, or a return character.

   The suggested word appears in place of the characters you typed.

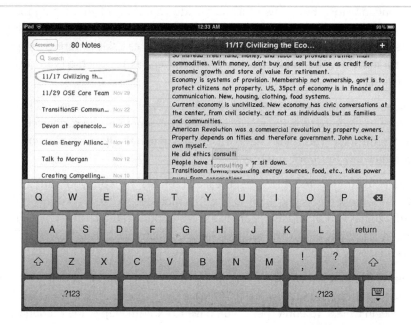

Figure 4.6 *The Dictionary suggests a completed or alternative version of the word you're typing.*

3. To begin to reject the suggested word, finish typing your word, but don't type a space, punctuation mark, or a return character.

   This is difficult, as you are probably in the habit of typing a space or other character without additional mental effort after typing a word. However, typing a space, punctuation mark, or return character replaces your word with the suggested word, which is not only frustrating, but also costs you an opportunity to retrain the Dictionary.

4. To finish rejecting the suggested word, tap the suggestion to dismiss it.

   The Dictionary notes both the word you actually entered and the word you rejected. It will now be more likely to accept your word in the future; the more times you reject the alternative in favor of "your" word, the more likely "your" word will be accepted going forward.

SHOW ME   Media 4.1—Working with Predictive Text
Access this video file through your registered Web Edition at
my.safaribooksonline.com/9780132709590/media
or on the DVD for print books.

You can turn auto-correction on or off; see Chapter 18, "Customizing Your iPad," for details. However, there is no option to leave auto-correction on, but not let it replace characters that you actually type with different characters. For instance, when I type "hella" and a space, I don't want that changed to hellas, overriding my space to end the word. When I type "hel" and a space, though, I might sometimes want that changed to Hellas.

Keyboards in Portrait Versus Landscape Mode

Each of the iPad's keyboards has two versions: portrait and landscape. Both versions have exactly the same keys; however, the keyboard is much bigger in landscape mode and takes up almost half the screen, as opposed to roughly one-fourth in portrait mode. See Figure 4.6 for an example of the keyboard in landscape mode.

This makes for an interesting trade-off. You may find that typing is more accurate in landscape mode; however, you can see so much less of the screen that you lose a lot of information. In some cases, for instance when entering text into a form on a web page, working in landscape mode can make it quite difficult to see what you're doing.

Holding the iPad in your hands, you can use either a portrait or landscape keyboard one-handed with your index finger or two-handed with your thumbs. When you set the iPad on your lap or your legs, on a desktop or tabletop, or put it in a stand, you may type with two hands, just as you can with a physical keyboard. (Although the iPad keyboard, even in landscape mode, is still only about half the area of the physical keyboard on a medium-sized laptop.)

Experiment to see how you work best. One optional piece of equipment that may help is the appropriate iPad case sold by Apple.

For the original iPad—now often called the "iPad 1" to differentiate it from the newer, thinner, lighter iPad 2—Apple sells the iPad Case, shown in Figure 4.7. The iPad Case has a clever notch that enables you to flip the back into it, creating a stand that makes the iPad work like an old-fashioned lap desk. (Lap desks date back to the precomputer days of relying on pen and paper, or even quill and ink.) The iPad Case works only in landscape mode; other cases and stands may support just one of the two modes or both modes.

For the iPad 2, Apple created the iPad Smart Cover. You have to see it in action to fully understand it—it's a flat cover, when placed on the iPad, that attaches via magnets to the edge of the device. However, the cover has four slats lengthwise across it, so you can roll it into a triangular shape, still attached to the iPad. You can use this triangular wedge as a kind of pillow for the long edge of the iPad, forming a different kind of "lap desk" than with the iPad Case for the original iPad.

Figure 4.7   *The iPad Case creates a small lap desk with your iPad front and center.*

Figure 4.8 shows the Smart Cover in use, but again, you really have to try it yourself to get the idea. I find the magnetic attachment too weak to use the "lap desk" alignment as flexibly as I'd like—sitting on a couch or sitting up in bed, for instance. It's very clever, though.

There's a bit of Steve Jobs lore that applies here, too. The Smart Cover leaves the back and edges of the iPad 2 exposed to scratches and scrapes. When asked about this, Jobs calls this kind of wear "weathering" and suggests that it makes the device more attractive, giving it character over time. It's a nice thought. If you don't agree, though, you may want to get a more traditional, full cover for the iPad 2.

Figure 4.8   *The Smart Cover for the iPad 2 is flexible and fun to use.*

Cutting, Copying, Pasting, and Defining Text

The iPad has been described as a device best suited for *consuming* information— for surfing Web pages, listening to music, and watching videos created by others. It's said to be much weaker for *creating* information—for writing, creating Web pages, drawing and painting onscreen, or creating audio or video.

Although the iPad is indeed excellent for consuming information, many new apps, including art apps with amazing capabilities, undermine this claim. However, the core question may be the iPad's capability to support rapid, accurate text entry. Even many multimedia works begin as a written email message and then are spelled out in a word processing document or even an Excel spreadsheet. If you can't enter and edit text and numbers on the iPad easily, its utility for creating any kind of information is undermined.

Fortunately, the iPad outperforms many people's expectations for text entry. Although entering text on a laptop, for instance, is easier, the iPad is quite adequate for the purpose. And the iPad has advantages that make it a viable option when the alternatives—most notably, a personal computer or handwritten notes— fail to perform adequately.

For example, my iPad is a great tool for taking notes in meetings. It's better than a paper notebook and pen because it's more efficient. In particular, I can easily take notes during a meeting, and then clean them up a bit and email them to participants immediately afterward.

Before the iPad, I often took notes on paper and then promised to transcribe them and email them afterward, but only managed it about half the time. With the iPad, this important (to me) task is easy.

This can be seen as a kind of "stupid pet trick," replacing a $5 paper notepad with an iPad that costs $500, minimum. At those prices, the iPad should, perhaps, do 100x more than the notepad. However, although not necessarily 100x better, the iPad is indeed a lot better. It saves time and effort and helps me get more done.

The iPad has many advantages over a laptop as well, including convenience, unobtrusiveness, light weight, and long battery life. There are many situations in which it's worth carrying an iPad, but wouldn't be worth carrying a laptop. One is at the airport—where, 10 years ago, Macs dominated business class, now you see more and more iPads.

The iPad is a great traveling companion. On a trip, whether for business or for pleasure, you might want to consider a few accessories. A pair of excellent, noise-canceling headphones, the Apple Wireless Keyboard, and the iPad Case (for the original iPad) or the iPad Smart Cover (for the iPad 2) top my list.

As mentioned earlier, the iPad is only roughly half as effective as a laptop or desktop computer for heavy work. However, its convenience and other advantages make it perfect for lighter demands. For this reason, many business travelers take the iPad on the plane and then continue with the iPad at their destinations, or alternate the iPad with a computer that travels as checked baggage on the flight. This approach definitely lightens the load and hassle of taking a laptop as part of carry-on luggage.

The Notes app is a great starting point for text work. For instance, given the vagaries of staying connected, I sometimes find it easier to compose a long email message in Notes, edit it, and then copy and paste the text into an email message before sending.

You also can easily define words with the iPad—a capability that was added in the Fall of 2011. Just select any single word. For most words, your iPad will offer a Define option alongside Cut, Copy, and Paste (or Replace). Tap Define to see a dictionary definition of the word. This is a fun and useful capability, and helps you disambiguate homonyms as well. (Which means, it helps you separate out words like "there" and "their", if you become uncertain as to which you need in a given spot.)

For all these uses, the ability to select, cut or copy, and then paste text are vital underpinnings to getting the most out of your iPad. Getting dictionary definitions of words is useful, too. Practice these tasks; your increased effectiveness can help you do more than others with your iPad.

TELL ME MORE   Media 4.2—Productivity on the iPad

Access this audio recording through your registered Web Edition at
my.safaribooksonline.com/9780132709590/media
or on the DVD for print books.

LET ME TRY IT

Cutting and Copying Text

1. Open the email message, Note, or other document that contains the text you want to select.

2. Display the text onscreen. If possible, rotate your iPad, scroll, and then zoom in to the extent that you can see the text you want to select and not much else.

3. Start the selection process. Tap and hold on the first word of text, if possible, or nearby, if not. For editable text, you also need to tap the Select button.

    The iPad displays the word as selected and shows selection handles around it, as shown in Figure 4.9. The left handle displays at the starting point of the selection; the right handle marks the end point.

4. Mark the end of the selection by dragging the handle of the endpoint of the selection to the right and down, as shown in Figure 4.10.
    As you drag the endpoint, the size of the selection increases.

5. If the text is not editable, as on a web page, you see a button above the text, Copy. (You can't Cut, because you can't edit the text.) If the text is editable, as in a Note or an email message, you see *two* buttons, Copy and Cut.

    Tap the corresponding button to copy or cut the text. You can copy or paste between applications. For instance, I sometimes copy the signature information from an email—name, address, phone number, and so on—and paste it into the Notes field of a contact, and then copy each piece from there into the appropriate field of the contact.

Start Point Handle

End Point Handle

Figure 4.9   *Tap and hold a word to display selection handles.*

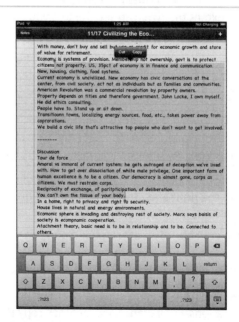

Figure 4.10   *Drag the endpoint selection handle to change the size of the selection.*

LET ME TRY IT

Pasting Text

1. Open the app and document—the email message, Note, or other document—that contains the spot where you want to paste text.

2. Tap to place the cursor where you want to insert the text. If you want to replace existing text with the pasted text, select the text you want to delete.

3. Tap the cursor. The iPad displays the buttons shown in Figure 4.11.

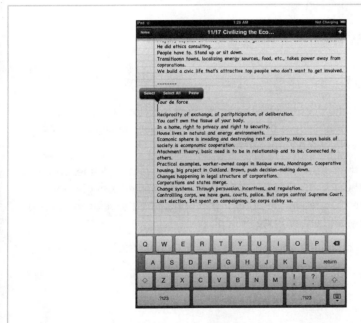

Figure 4.11   *Tap the cursor and then tap Paste to paste selected text.*

4. Tap Paste. The iPad pastes the selected text into the selected spot or replaces the selected text with the pasted text.

Here's a gesture for you: to undo pasting, shake your iPad. The Undo Paste command appears; tap it to select it. The paste operation will be reversed. Then, explain to the people around you why you were shaking your iPad!

5. If the text is not editable, as on a web page, you see a Copy button above the text. If the text is editable, as in a Note or an email message, you see *two* buttons: Copy and Cut.

   Tap a corresponding button to copy or cut the text.

SHOW ME   Media 4.3—Copying and Pasting Text
Access this video file through your registered Web Edition at
my.safaribooksonline.com/9780132709590/media
or on the DVD for print books.

LET ME TRY IT

Defining a Word

1. Open the app and document—the email message, Note, or other document—that contains the spot where you want to get the definition of a word. Or, type the word whose definition you want to get.

2. Tap to place the cursor in or next to the word you want to define. Choose Select from the options that appear. If you have selected a single word, Define will be included in the options that appear for the selection (alongside Cut, Copy, and either Paste or Replace).

3. Tap Define. A definition appears, as shown in Figure 4.12.

4. Tap anywhere to clear the definition.

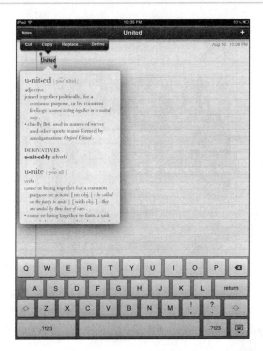

Figure 4.12   *Tap Define to see a dictionary definition of the selected word.*

Copying and Pasting Images

Belying its reputation for being creatively limited, the iPad makes it easy to copy and paste images.

 LET ME TRY IT

Copying and Pasting an Image

1. Find an image that you want to copy and tap and hold it.

   Options appear, as shown in Figure 4.13.

2. Tap Copy. The iPad stores a copy of the image in memory.

3. Open the app and, if applicable, the document where you want to paste the image, similar to the steps provided in Pasting Text, in the previous section.

Figure 4.13   *Tapping on an image gives you options.*

4. Position the cursor at the exact location where you want the image to appear.

   It may be hard to move the image after you paste it, so it's worthwhile to position the insertion point carefully instead.

5. Tap the cursor. Your iPad gives you options, including Paste.

6. Tap Paste. Your iPad pastes the image into the selected location. To undo the paste, shake your iPad, just as you can do after pasting text.

In this chapter, you learn how to synchronize your iPad with your personal computer for music, movies, TV shows, games, and more.

5

Syncing Your iPad

Apple has long been criticized for making the iPhone and now the iPad dependent on synchronization to a computer for updates and managing media. However, this dependence is gradually fading.

You need to synchronize your iPad when you first get it for updates to the operating system. It's also easier to search for and download content into iTunes on your personal computer. That's because the computer is likely to have a faster connection, bigger screen, and bigger hard disk. Even some iPad apps and upgrades won't download directly to the iPad; they need to go to iTunes on your computer first and then be transferred through synchronization.

However, you can get a lot of content and most apps for your iPad directly. When you connect your iPad to your computer, the two devices synchronize their content.

You can also stream movies, videos, and sound files from a personal computer running iTunes to an iPad as long as both the computer and the iPad are on the same wireless network. This can greatly reduce your need to move files onto the iPad in the first place. For details, see Chapter 12, "Managing Music on Your iPad," and Chapter 16, "Importing and Viewing Video Clips."

You'll be familiar with much of this if you own an iPhone, iPod Touch, or other iPod, in which case you'll already be quite familiar with iTunes. What's different with the iPad is that because of its larger screen, you will probably want to do a lot more with movies and video, including purchased and rented content. The iPad is a great device for watching videos and movies.

Movie and video files are many gigabytes (GB) in size—half a gigabyte for a one-hour, standard definition television show; 3GB to 4GB for a typical two-hour movie, and more for high-definition (HD) movies and for extras that come with many movies you might purchase. These files are far, far bigger than books or songs, which take only about 3MB each. (Although some of you may have song libraries that add up to a gigabyte or more in size.) Your iPad can certainly overfill if you use much video, especially if you have one of the smaller-capacity models, at 16GB or even 32GB.

TV and movie files are so big that you might find it a challenge to store them even on your computer's hard disk, let alone on your iPad. Consider getting an external hard drive or other additional storage to hold your video library on your computer, giving you a bigger well of content to selectively transfer to your iPad.

This chapter and other parts of this book focus on using iTunes on your computer first because it's probably the best and easiest place to snarf up and store all sorts of content. (Especially with the streaming capability over Wi-Fi available.)

It's also good to use your computer as a storage resource for other devices besides your iPad, such as your mobile phone—whether that's an iPhone, an Android phone, a BlackBerry, a Nokia, or some other popular model.

In this chapter, you learn how to transfer content and apps mostly one-way, from your computer to your iPad—and selectively, so you can keep a big library on your computer and copy only what you currently need to your iPad. (The same logic applies to other devices, such as a mobile phone.) Don't be afraid to bring content and apps directly onto your iPad first, though; they'll be copied back to your computer the next time you synchronize, a relatively quick process.

Understanding Synchronizing

Synchronizing is usually understood to mean getting two devices to have the exact same settings and content. The phrase "synchronize your watches" means getting two or more watches onto the same time setting.

However, synchronizing has a more specific meaning for your iPad and your computer. It means copying selected information and settings back and forth in a way in which you specify. The end result is that selected information and settings are the same on both devices.

Two things happen when you synchronize your iPad with your computer:

- Information that you download into iTunes gets copied to your iPad. This includes media files, such as movies, videos, songs, and photos, and personal information manager (PIM)-type files, such as calendar items, contacts, and appointments.

ⓖ   *For Information about synchronizing email, calendars, and contact information, see Chapter 6, "Setting Up Email."*

- Information that you download onto your iPad gets copied back to your computer. This can also include media files and PIM-type files.

By keeping your iPad and your computer in sync, you should have the data you need handy on either device when you need it. The iPad usually has a subset of your computer's data, though, so you need to manage your synchronization settings carefully to have the best chance to have the data you need on your iPad when you need it.

For instance, if you have an entire year's worth of shows from a TV series on your computer but copy only a few shows onto your iPad to save room, you can easily run out of shows to watch on your iPad—during a trip, for instance—even though you've paid for the entire season and have it available on your computer.

If you use a cloud-based service, such as Google services or Apple's Mobile Me, for PIM-type information, this information might be constantly updated via wireless connections. It doesn't depend on a specific synchronization operation carried out by connecting the iPad to a computer.

 TELL ME MORE   Media 5.1—Syncing Movies and Video
Access this audio recording through your registered Web Edition at
my.safaribooksonline.com/9780132709590/media
or on the DVD for print books.

Synchronizing Your iPad and Your Computer

Your iPad and your computer automatically synchronize as soon as you connect them. As soon as your computer detects that the iPad is connected, it opens iTunes, and iTunes drives the synchronization process.

Performance of both your iPad and your personal computer is likely to suffer during synchronization. Both devices are very busy transferring and saving files at this time, and your additional demands just annoy them. Consider carefully what kind of tasks you'll be doing and whether they can wait a little while before starting a synchronization process.

You can connect your iPad directly to your computer via the USB port on your computer and the multipurpose port on the bottom of your iPad, or you can set your iPad on a stand that connects to your computer in the same manner.

Unfortunately, many USB ports are not sufficiently high-powered to charge your iPad during synchronization—or any other time either. If this is the case for you, you usually need your iPad connected directly to a power source to recharge or to maintain a charge much of the time. Connecting to a USB port for synchronization can be something you do less frequently.

Using the iPad's wall socket connector is always the best choice when available. It's fastest and made for the purpose—and it's easily replaced if there's a problem. If you wear out the USB port on your computer, on the other hand, it's expensive and a hassle to replace it.

By default, iTunes only includes only a subset of the data it has at hand for synchronization with the iPad. For best results, you need to tell iTunes exactly what you want synced and to vary this depending on what content you obtain and the capacity of your iPad. The later chapters in this book include specifics on how to synchronize various kinds of data.

⊙ *For details on synchronizing movies between your computer and your iPad, see "Synchronizing Video Clips" in Chapter 16.*

The basic procedure for setting up your iPad for syncing is shown here.

SHOW ME   Media 5.2—Syncing Your iPad with Your Computer
Access this video file through your registered Web Edition at
my.safaribooksonline.com/9780132709590/media
or on the DVD for print books.

LET ME TRY IT

Syncing Your iPad and Your Computer

1. Connect your iPad to your Windows PC or Mac via USB. Wait while iTunes loads and recognizes your iPad, which might take a little while.

2. In the iTunes sidebar, click your iPad in the Devices branch. iTunes displays the Summary tab, as shown in Figure 5.1.

3. Use the other tabs, such as Apps, Movies, and TV Shows, to choose the data you want to synchronize.

   See the relevant chapters in this book to learn the details about each tab.

4. Click Apply.

   iTunes synchronizes data between your computer and your iPad. While the sync is in progress, you see the screen shown in Figure 5.2 on your iPad. You can't use your iPad until the sync completes unless you use the slider to cancel the sync operation.

5. When the sync is complete, click the Eject icon next to your iPad's name in the Devices list (refer to Figure 5.1).

Figure 5.1   *Click your iPad in the Devices list to see this Summary tab.*

Figure 5.2   *Your iPad displays this screen while iPad syncs it with your computer.*

Wireless Sync for Your iPad

Apple began supporting wireless synchronization for iOS devices—the iPad, iPhones, and the iPod Touch—with the release of iOS 5 in Fall 2011. To sync wirelessly, both your computer and your iPad need to be connected to the same wireless network.

Wireless syncing is a bit slower than syncing over USB. There's also some danger of your iPad overfilling with content if you have a lot of content and aren't careful about setting your options.

However, syncing wirelessly is convenient and easy, once you get it set up. You just plug your iPad into a power source, and it's available for updating. If you have automatic syncing set up, you don't have to do anything more—it just starts.

You do have to get it set up, though. This involves physically connecting your iPad to your computer as a first step—although you may never have to physically connect the two again!

After you set the syncing options, as described in the steps in the next section, your iPad is available for syncing any time you plug it into a power source.

 LET ME TRY IT

Syncing Your iPad and Your Computer

1. Connect your iPad to your Windows PC or Mac via USB. Wait while iTunes loads and recognizes your iPad, which might take a little while.

2. In the iTunes sidebar, click your iPad in the Devices branch. iTunes displays the Summary tab, as shown in Figure 5.3.

3. Set relevant options: Sync over Wi-Fi connection (required) and Manually manage music and videos (optional). Click Apply.

   The options are applied.

4. Disconnect your iPad from the computer and plug it into a power source.

   Your iPad appears in the Devices branch in iTunes. If you did not set the option Manually manage music and videos, your iPad will begin syncing.

5. If you set the option Manually manage music and videos, then drag content from within the various content tabs in iTunes onto your iPad in the devices tab.

   The content will be copied to your iPad wirelessly.

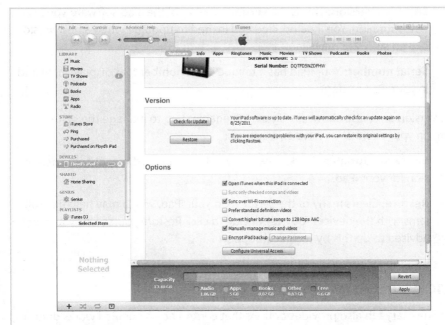

Figure 5.3 *Set options for wireless syncing—and you may never connect your iPad to your computer again!*

Setting the Summary Options in iTunes

When you select your iPad from the Devices list in iTunes, iTunes provides tabs for specific types of data and a Summary tab for general settings that apply to all synchronization activities. The next section describes what's on the Summary tab and how to manage those settings. Later chapters describe the remaining tabs and the type of information they manage, such as info, apps, and so on.

Understanding Version Options

The Summary tab provides information about your iPad and options for its system software (refer to Figure 5.1). The information provided includes the following:

- **Name:** The name of your device. You can change this by clicking your device's name in the Devices list and typing a new name.

- **Capacity:** This is the total amount of available storage space on your iPad before you copy any data to it, but not including the space needed for system software. The system software takes up about 2GB, whether you have a 16GB, 32GB, or 64GB iPad. So the remaining space will be about 14GB, 30GB, or 62GB.

- **Software version:** This is the version number of the iPad software you're currently running. You'll be notified and invited to upgrade when a new version of iPad software is available.

- **Serial number:** Your iPad has a unique serial number that displays here and in your iPad settings.

The Version area, also shown in Figure 5.3, enables you to manage the system software on your device. You have two options:

- **Check for Update:** Checks whether you have the most recent software version for your iPad.

- **Restore:** Clears many of the settings on your iPad, which may help fix problems with the device. You may decide to click Restore yourself, or you may be advised to do this by technical support.

Using Summary Options

The Summary tab also provides options that control how your iPad works during synchronization, as shown previously in Figure 5.3.

The options include

- **Open iTunes When This iPad Is Connected:** iTunes opens, and synchronization begins whenever your computer detects that your iPad is newly connected to it. Clear this option to put iTunes launch under manual control.

- **Sync Only Checked Songs and Videos:** iTunes syncs only songs and videos checked in your iTunes library when syncing.

- **Prefer Standard Definition Videos:** By default, iPad prefers High Definition (HD) videos, when both HD and standard video versions are available, when syncing videos to your iPad. Select this option to prefer standard definition videos instead. This saves storage space on your iPad at a slight loss in the quality you perceive. (Much of the quality advantage of an HD video may not be all that visible or audible on an iPad anyway.)

- **Convert Higher Bit Rate Songs to 128 kbps AAC:** Downsizes audio files to 128kbps AAC format when transferring them to your iPad, which reduces the amount of storage space the file takes up, with some loss of quality. The loss in quality may not be very audible unless you have higher-end speakers or headphones for use with your iPad.

- **Manually Manage Music and Videos:** Turns off automatic syncing for music and videos. Use settings in the Music and Video settings panes to manage syncing instead.

- **Encrypt iPad Backup:** iTunes backs up the information on your iPad to your computer when you synchronize. Check this option to encrypt the backup. If you choose it, you'll be asked for a password. You need the password to restore the information to your iPad. After a password is set, click the Change Password button to change the password.

- **Configure Universal Access:** Turns on accessibility options such as VoiceOver and Zoom. See iTunes Help for more information.

iTunes automatically backs up your device when you sync, and the backup can be a great time-saver. Not only does it help you if something goes wrong with a given device, but you can also use the backup to help you initialize a new device. You can also synchronize a new iPad to a backup of an old one and synchronize a new iPad to a backup of an iPhone! This is useful for many purposes; however, after the iPhone-to-iPad transfer, you'll want to look for iPad-specific versions of as many of the iPhone apps you've inherited as possible.

 SHOW ME   Media 5.3—Managing Storage Settings on Your iPad
Access this video file through your registered Web Edition at
my.safaribooksonline.com/9780132709590/media
or on the DVD for print books.

In this chapter you learn how to set up various email accounts to work within the Mail app on your iPad and how to synchronize associated contact and calendar information.

6

Setting Up Email

Smoothly managing email is one of the great challenges of using computers and mobile devices. When it works well, your life is made easier, more productive, and more fun. When it doesn't, confusion and frustration may follow.

The iPad is a great device for handling email. Because you can carry it with you, you can keep up on email around the house or on the go. With the iPad's large screen, you can see what you're doing without squinting and see more of a message without scrolling.

Using touch to find, open, and respond to emails is fun. Interacting so directly with your mail is a bit like the satisfying feeling of dealing with paper mail but without the mess or the wasted paper.

Typing on the iPad is slower than typing from the physical keyboard on a computer but not unacceptably slow. You might decide to type shorter messages on your iPad and save the longer efforts for your computer.

Your iPad's Mail app can combine email from several different accounts. You can set it to download email from your computer or to sync to a cloud-based service such as Gmail or your work email.

Your iPad can download and send messages only when it's connected to the Internet, but you can still access stored messages and create new messages when you're not connected. Your iPad syncs up again when you get an Internet connection.

Along with your email, you can, for some types of accounts, also synchronize your contacts and calendar information. This makes your iPad even more powerful as a tool for working with more of your important information.

So in setting up one or more email accounts on your iPad, you can increase convenience and have fun—all without sacrificing your normal techniques for managing email and, perhaps, related data. This is a good thing to keep in mind as you proceed.

The iPad works as a "downstream" email device. When you delete an email from your iPad, it isn't deleted from the host email account—just from your iPad. When you write and send an email from your iPad, it's copied to the host email account, so you can file, forward, or otherwise deal with it further from there.

Synchronizing Email Accounts with iTunes

You probably already use at least one email account, and you might juggle several different ones. You might even have different email accounts on different devices. For instance, many workplaces won't allow cloud-based email accounts such as Yahoo! Mail or Gmail to be used on work machines. So employees have to bring in personal mobile phones—or, now, an iPad—to keep up with their personal email. The iPad enables you to combine different kinds of email accounts on one convenient device.

You can create an email account directly on your iPad, as described in the next section, but it's easier to use iTunes to synchronize your email account with your iPad.

 LET ME TRY IT

Synchronizing Email Accounts

1. Connect your iPad to your Mac or Windows PC.

2. In the iTunes sidebar, click your iPad in the Devices branch. iTunes displays the Summary tab for your iPad.

3. Click the Info tab.

4. If you use a Windows PC, select the Sync Mail Accounts From check box. Use the list that appears to select your Windows email program, as shown in Figure 6.1. If you use a Mac, click to select the Sync Mail Accounts check box.

5. Click the check box beside each mail account that you want to synchronize with your iPad.

6. Click Apply. iTunes synchronizes the email accounts you selected from your computer to your iPad. (Only account settings, not mail messages, synchronize at this point. To manage messages, use the Mail settings on your iPad, as described in the next section.)

7. When synchronization is complete, click the Eject icon next to your iPad's name in the iTunes Devices list.

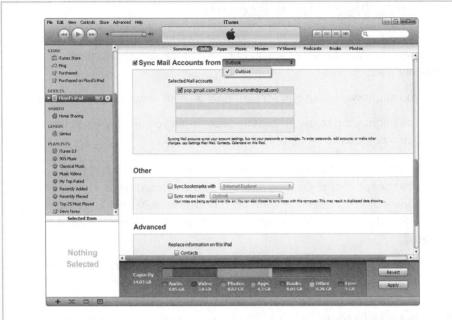

Figure 6.1 *On your Windows PC, activate the Sync Mail Accounts check box.*

 TELL ME MORE Media 6.1—Understanding Different Email Account Options

Access this audio recording through your registered Web Edition at my.safaribooksonline.com/9780132709590/media or on the DVD for print books.

Working with Email Accounts

In addition to managing email accounts for your iPad in iTunes, as described in the previous section, you can work with email accounts directly on your iPad. You can create a new email account and edit or delete existing email accounts. The next few sections have the details.

After you add one or more email accounts to your iPad using iTunes or by adding the accounts directly, as described here, mail from each account shows up in the Mail application. You can read, reply to, and delete messages. Your replies are copied to the email account, and deleting messages deletes them only from the iPad, not from the main copy of the email account.

Creating a New Email Account

It's easy to get email accounts onto your iPad by synchronizing them from your Windows PC or Mac. However, you might want to manage the account directly from your iPad:

- You might want to use an account only on your iPad, not on your computer.
- You might want to use an existing account on your iPad when you're not near your computer to synchronize it with your iPad.

You can use your iPad to create the email account directly. The following sections show you the specifics of creating all seven of the account types supported by the iPad: Apple's MobileMe service; Webmail services Gmail, Yahoo!, and AOL Mail; and Microsoft Exchange, POP (Post Office Protocol), and IMAP (Internet Message Access Protocol).

If your specific email service, such as Hotmail, is not listed here, you can set it up to synchronize as either a POP or IMAP account.

 TELL ME MORE   Media 6.2—Understanding POP and IMAP Email Accounts

Access this audio recording through your registered Web Edition at
my.safaribooksonline.com/9780132709590/media
or on the DVD for print books.

Creating a New MobileMe Account

MobileMe is an online service offered by Apple. It's a cloud-based service, meaning that the core copies of your email, contact, and calendar information reside on Internet servers, not on your Macintosh or other computer. It's quite capable and includes 20GB of online storage, hosting or basic Web pages, and other cool features.

At this writing, MobileMe is a paid service and is popular mainly among Macintosh users. It has received good reviews and has excellent alignment between a Macintosh, iPad, and iPhone. However, it competes with services such as Gmail and Yahoo! that offer similar capabilities for free.

Follow these steps to configure MobileMe from your iPad:

1. From the iPad Home screen, tap Settings; then tap Mail > Contacts > Calendars.

2. Tap Add Account.

3. Tap the MobileMe logo.

4. Enter your information in the AppleID and Password boxes, as shown in Figure 6.2.

Figure 6.2 *Enter your name, address, password, and optional description for MobileMe.*

5. Optionally, use the Description box to enter a short description of the account.

6. Tap the Next button. Your iPad contacts the MobileMe service to verify your account. It then displays the MobileMe screen, which lists the data you can sync between your MobileMe account and the iPad.

Figure 6.3   *Synchronize mail and, if available, contacts, calendars, bookmarks, and notes.*

7. Set the Mail switch to On. You can also set switches to On to synchronize Contacts, Calendars, Bookmarks, and Notes.

8. Tap Save. Your mail and other selected information will be synchronized with your iPad.

You may or may not see a Find My iPad slider. If so, you can turn it on as a service within MobileMe. However, the Find My iPad service is now available to all users— not just MobileMe customers—as a free app.

 LET ME TRY IT

Creating a New Gmail Account

Gmail is one of the most popular services for not only email, but also for contacts and calendar information. It is cloud-based, so the core copies of your email, contact, and calendar information reside on Internet servers, not on your computer. Gmail is known for offering the most free storage of any free cloud-based mail account, more than 7GB at this writing. (This sounds like a lot, but after four years of what seems to me like moderate use of Gmail, I'm using 4GB of space.)

You can get an increase in storage for Gmail, to 25GB, and many other features, by getting a Google Apps account. The current cost is $50 per year.

Follow these steps to configure Gmail from your iPad:

1. From the iPad Home screen, tap Settings; then tap Mail > Contacts > Calendars.

2. Tap Add Account.

3. Tap the Gmail logo.

4. Enter your information in the Name, Address, and Password boxes.

5. Optionally, use the Description box to enter a short description of the account.

6. Tap the Next button. Your iPad contacts Google to verify your account. It then displays the Gmail screen shown in [Figure 6.4, which lists the data you can sync between your Gmail account and the iPad.

Figure 6.4   *Synchronize Gmail mail and, if you want, calendars and contacts.*

7. Set the Mail switch to On. You can also set switches to On to synchronize Calendars and Notes.

8. Tap Save. Your mail and other selected information synchronize with your iPad.

If you are a Gmail user, consider using the Gmail app for the iPad; it has strong search capabilities. If Gmail is your only email account, you might want to use the Gmail app instead of the native iPad Mail app; however, it's the Mail app that's used as the mailing function for the built-in Notepad app and possibly other apps. You can also use Gmail as a kind of traffic cop for email from all sorts of different accounts. However, it's probably easier to bring multiple email accounts into Mail, as described in this chapter, to unify your email. You might want to download the Gmail app and use it occasionally, though, for its strong abilities to search your Gmail messages.

 **LET ME TRY IT**

Creating a New Yahoo! Mail Account

Yahoo! Mail still has a great deal of loyalty among its tens of millions of users. Like MobileMe and Gmail, Yahoo! Mail is cloud-based—the core copies of your email, contact, and calendar information reside on Internet servers, not on your computer. Yahoo! Mail recently increased its storage limit to 1GB. This is a lot of data but still small enough that you probably want to fully delete "junk" email—and any email with large attachments that you don't really need to keep—from your account.

To configure Yahoo! Mail from your iPad, follow these steps:

1. From the iPad Home screen, tap Settings; then tap Mail > Contacts > Calendars.

2. Tap Add Account.

3. Tap the Yahoo! logo.

4. Enter your information in the Name, Address, and Password boxes.

5. Optionally, use the Description box to enter a short description of the account.

6. Tap the Next button. Your iPad contacts Yahoo! to verify your account. It then displays the Yahoo! screen shown in Figure 6.5, which lists the data you can sync between your Yahoo! account and the iPad.

Figure 6.5   *Synchronize Yahoo! Mail and, optionally, calendars and contacts.*

7. Set the Mail switch to On. You can also set switches to On to synchronize Calendars and Notes.

8. Tap Save. Your mail and other selected information synchronize with your iPad.

 LET ME TRY IT

Creating a New AOL Mail Account

AOL Mail was extremely popular in the 1990s and still retains millions of users. Many users pay AOL money every month just to retain their @aol.com email address, with AOL's strong spam protection. As with the other services listed here, AOL email is cloud-based—the core copies of your email reside on Internet servers, not on your computer. AOL email has limitations on Inbox size, but you can move an unlimited amount of email to folders. Your iPad only syncs AOL email and n otes, not calendar information. This is a big limitation, as you then have to find some other way to do your calendar and, if desired, keep it synchronized across platforms.

To configure AOL Mail from your iPad, follow these steps:

1. From the iPad Home screen, tap Settings; then tap Mail > Contacts > Calendars.

2. Tap Add Account.

3. Tap the AOL logo.

4. Enter your information in the Name, Address, and Password boxes.

5. Optionally, use the Description box to enter a short description of the account.

6. Tap the Next button. Your iPad contacts AOL to verify your account. It then displays the AOL screen shown in Figure 6.6, which lists the data you can sync between your AOL account and the iPad.

Figure 6.6   *Synchronize AOL Mail and, optionally, notes.*

7. Set the Mail switch to On. You can also set switches to On to synchronize Notes.

8. Tap Save. Your mail and notes if selected synchronize with your iPad.

 **LET ME TRY IT**

Creating a New Microsoft Exchange Account

Microsoft Exchange is the backbone of a large number of business email accounts. If you want to synchronize your iPad with a business email account, you're likely to use Microsoft Exchange to do so.

For an Exchange account, you might need to enter information that you don't normally use—your Exchange domain name, if you have one, and your account username (in addition to your email address). You also need to enter your password, which is typical for email account setup, but which you might not know if you routinely access your work email through a computer and/or mobile phone (typically a BlackBerry) in which this information has been pre-entered for you.

Contact your technical support department at work early if you think you might need help getting needed information to set up a Microsoft Exchange account on your iPad. Get your Exchange domain name (if any), Exchange server name (if any), and Exchange account username and password if you don't already have them. Get tech support to walk you through the process if possible. Also check company policies for accessing, storing, and sending work email from devices not issued by your company; it could be against the rules.

Email storage policies in organizations differ, but many organizations still have strict limits on the size of your Inbox. Use other accounts, such as one of the cloud-based accounts described in the previous sections, for personal messages. Find out about such limitations early and work to keep your storage from running up against limits. Otherwise your account could reject important incoming messages at inopportune times, such as while you're on vacation and can't fix the problem quickly.

Follow these steps to configure a Microsoft Exchange account from your iPad:

1. From the iPad Home screen, tap Settings; then tap Mail > Contacts > Calendars.

2. Tap Add Account.

3. Tap the Microsoft Exchange logo.

4. Enter your Exchange email address in the Email box.

5. Enter your Exchange domain name (if any) in the Domain box, as shown in Figure 6.7. You might have to contact technical support at your work to find out if you have a domain name and to get the name if you do have one.

> Gmail uses Exchange for synchronization through the cloud. For instructions, see Help for your Gmail account. For other types of email, check the service's Help to see if it uses Exchange for the same purpose. The iPad used to limit you to one Exchange-based email setup per user, but that limitation was removed with the launch of iOS 4.2 late in 2010.

Cancel	Account	Done

Email	floydearlsmith@gmail.com
Server	m.google.com

Domain	Optional
Username	floydearlsmith@gmail.com
Password	••••••••

Description	floydearlsmith@gmail.com

Use SSL	ON

Figure 6.7   *Enter the information needed for your Exchange account—Gmail shown here.*

6. Enter your Exchange account username in the Username box.

7. Enter your Exchange account password in the Password box.

8. Optionally, use the Description box to enter a short description of the account.

9. Tap the Next button. Your iPad contacts the Exchange server to verify your account. If it can't verify the account, your iPad might display an updated screen, requesting the name of your Exchange server. Enter the server

name (which you might need to get from your company's technical support team) in the Server box. Your iPad then displays the Exchange screen, which lists the data you can sync between your Microsoft Exchange account and the iPad.

10. Set the Mail switch to On. You can also set switches to On to synchronize Contacts and Calendars, as shown in Figure 6.8.

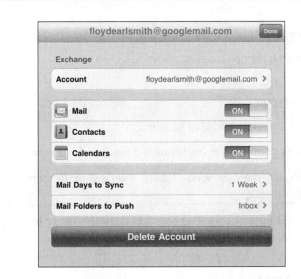

Figure 6.8   *Sync your Exchange account to make your iPad a power tool.*

11. Tap Save. Your mail, and contacts and calendars if selected, synchronize with your iPad.

 LET ME TRY IT

Creating a New IMAP Account

Your iPad supports many types of mail accounts directly, as described in the previous sections. However, there are additional types of email that it does not support directly, including Web-based services such as Microsoft Hotmail and Live Mail. For types of email accounts not directly supported, you can choose either IMAP or POP support.

For email synchronization, IMAP attempts full synchronization between a target device and the email host, supporting deletions, for instance, across all platforms. POP, the older standard, is more targeted toward downloading mail from a host to a target device, not necessarily fully synchronizing deletions, for instance. POP, though older, is somewhat more reliable and is more in keeping with the spirit of the iPad's approach to email. Consider trying both IMAP and POP to find the best fit for the way you use email on your iPad.

Follow these steps to configure an email account on your iPad using IMAP support:

1. From the iPad Home screen, tap Settings; then tap Mail > Contacts > Calendars.

2. Tap Add Account.

3. Tap Other. Then tap Add Mail Account.

4. Enter your information in the Name, Address, and Password boxes.

5. Optionally, use the Description box to enter a short description of the account.

6. Tap the Next button. Your iPad contacts the IMAP server to verify your account and then adds the account.

 LET ME TRY IT

Creating a New POP Account

For email account types that your iPad does not support directly, you can choose IMAP or POP support. Some email accounts don't support IMAP, leaving POP as the only choice. However, even if you have a choice of both, you might want to choose POP. Though it doesn't synchronize deletions, for instance, as IMAP does, POP is simple and reliable. It puts new emails onto your iPad, where you can do with them as you please—leaving the main copy of your emails on a server or another computer, undisturbed.

To set up a POP account, you need to configure an outgoing message server and an incoming one. Therefore, to set up a POP account, you need to know not only your email address and account password, but also the hostnames of your provider's incoming and outgoing message servers. Find this information out from your email provider.

Follow these steps to configure a POP account on your iPad:

1. From the iPad Home screen, tap Settings; then tap Mail > Contacts > Calendars.

2. Tap Add Account.

3. Tap Other. Then tap Add Mail Account.

4. Enter your information in the Name, Address, and Password boxes.

5. Optionally, use the Description box to enter a short description of the account.

6. Tap the Next button. Your iPad tries to verify the account data but fails and then displays the Enter Your Account screen.

7. Tap POP. In the Incoming Mail Server section, enter the incoming mail server in the Host Name box and your username and password. In the Outgoing Mail Server section, enter the *outgoing* mail server in the Host Name box and if requested, your username and password.

8. Tap Save. Your iPad verifies the account information and adds the account.

Editing Email Accounts

You might want to make changes to an account after you've added it, whether through iTunes or directly from your iPad. You can change the display name to help you quickly find the right account; the account description; or, for some kinds of accounts, which data gets synchronized to your iPad. You also want to set and might want to change which email account is used as the default email account for the Mail app.

 SHOW ME   Media 6.3—Editing Email Accounts
Access this video file through your registered Web Edition at
my.safaribooksonline.com/9780132709590/media
or on the DVD for print books.

 LET ME TRY IT

Setting the Default Mail Account

If you use more than one email account with your iPad, follow these steps to set the default mail account:

1. From the iPad Home screen, tap Settings; then tap Mail > Contacts > Calendars.

2. Tap Default Account.

3. Tap the account you want to use as the default.

 LET ME TRY IT

Editing An Email Account

Follow these steps to edit an email account that you've added:

1. From the iPad Home screen, tap Settings; then tap Mail > Contacts > Calendars.

2. Tap the account you want to edit.

3. For accounts that have varying synchronization settings for different types of data, you can use the initial screen to change the settings. Move the appropriate slider to turn synchronization on or off for a specific type of data.

4. To edit account data, such as the account name or account description, tap Account Info. Then edit the account data as required.

5. Tap Done. Your iPad saves the account data.

 LET ME TRY IT

Deleting an Email Account

You might want to remove an email account from the iPad at some point. Follow these steps to do so:

1. From the iPad Home screen, tap Settings; then tap Mail > Contacts > Calendars.

2. Tap the account you want to delete.

3. At the bottom of the screen, tap Delete Account. Your iPad asks you to confirm the deletion.

4. Tap Delete Account.

In this chapter you learn how to send and receive
email messages on your iPad.

7

Handling Notifications and Email Messages

When you have email accounts set up properly, as described in Chapter 6, "Setting Up Email," you can use your iPad's Mail app to send and receive email messages. You can even send email messages from other apps that support the capability, such as the Notes app.

In the Notes app, you can send a note that you create as an email message, making it easy to share items such as meeting notes. You can also email the notes to yourself for further work before you forward them to others.

 TELL ME MORE   Media 7.1—Email on the iPad Versus a Computer
Access this audio recording through your registered Web Edition at
my.safaribooksonline.com/9780132709590/media
or on the DVD for print books.

Sending Email Messages

When you have one or more email accounts configured on your iPad, you're ready to exchange messages with friends and family and with all kinds of companies, service providers, and others.

It's easy to create new messages, and your iPad even provides a customizable signature for your messages. The default custom signature is Sent from my iPad, but you can easily change it, as described later in the section "Customizing Your Email Signature."

You can send email messages from within some apps and also from within some Web pages. After you've successfully created and sent an email message from the Mail app, as described here, try sending an email message from within Notes. Steps to do so are described in the section, "Taking Notes," in Chapter 17, "Working with Apps and the App Store." You can also email a photo from the Photos app, as described in the section, "Emailing a Photo," in Chapter 15, "Importing and Viewing Photos."

LET ME TRY IT

Creating and Sending an Email Message

Follow these steps to create and send an email message:

1. On the Home screen, tap Mail to launch the Mail app.

   If the iPad is in landscape (horizontal) mode, the Inbox for your default email account displays. If it's in portrait (vertical) mode, tap the Inbox button to see your messages, as shown in Figure 7.1.

2. If you have multiple email accounts configured and you want to send the email from a different account and continue using that account, tap the button with your account name in the Inbox. If you want to use the account that's currently chosen, skip to Step 4.

   The Mail app displays the Mailboxes screen.

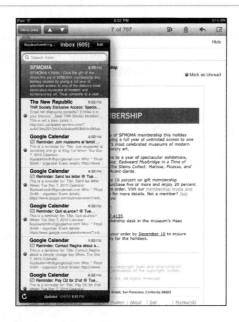

Figure 7.1   *In portrait mode, tap the Inbox button to see incoming email messages.*

3. Tap the account you want to use to send the message.

   The Mail app now displays the Inbox for that account.

4. Tap the New Message icon.

A new message appears onscreen, as shown in Figure 7.2.

Figure 7.2 *You have lots of options with new messages.*

5. Tap in the To field.

A plus symbol (+) appears on the right side of the To field.

6. Enter the recipients. You can type the email address directly, either just the email address (that is, budsmith@gmail.com) or a name and an email address (that is, Bud Smith <budsmith@gmail.com>). As you type, the Mail app displays a list of previously used email addresses, from which you can select. You can also select a recipient directly from your Contacts by tapping the + button and choosing the appropriate contact.
The recipient appears in the To: list.

7. If you want, enter additional email recipients—either directly or by using the Add button to select from your contacts.

8. If you want to enter carbon copy (cc) and blind carbon copy (bcc) recipients, tap the Cc:Bcc field and then enter additional recipients directly or use the Add button to select from your contacts.

Direct recipients of your message (in the To: list) and copied recipients (in the Cc: list) see one another's names along with your message. They don't see the names of recipients who are blind-copied (in the Bcc: list).

Blind-copied recipients (in the Bcc: list) see the names of recipients in the To: and Cc: lists, but they do not see other blind-copied recipients.

If someone taps Reply All to respond to your email, recipients in the To: list and the Cc: list receive the reply, but not recipients in the Bcc: list. This happens even if it's someone in the Bcc: list who uses Reply All.

Recipients in the Bcc: list don't receive replies sent using Reply All. So using Bcc: is a popular way to prevent replies from going to too many people and to people who are unlikely to be interested in the reply.

9. Tap the Subject field and then enter a subject line for your message.

10. Tap in the large text area below the Subject field and then enter the body of your message.

    You can copy and paste text and images from other programs, such as the Notes app or the Photos app, into an email message.

    To save a draft of the message, press the Cancel button. You'll then be offered a choice to press the Delete Draft button or the Save Draft button. If you press Save Draft, the message is saved in the Drafts folder.

    Composing an email message in another program, such as the Notes app, can be a good way to take your time with composing the text of a message without interfering with your ability to juggle incoming emails.

11. Tap Send.

    The mail app sends your message.

Rich Text in Email Messages

One of the biggest advances in email on computers has been the increasing use of rich text for email messages. "Rich text" just means text with effects like fonts, bolding, italics, bulleted lists, and so on.

Rich text is great for email because it fits the way people read on an electronic device. Reading from a screen has been compared to staring into a light bulb. It's harder than reading from paper—although that doesn't stop people from doing it.

However, people comprehend less when they read from a backlit screen. They tend to read for shorter stretches of time, to skim, and to remember less.

One partial antidote for these tendencies is rich text. By using headers, bold and italic, and bulleted lists, among other effects, text becomes easier to scan. High points can be made stronger, and blocks of text can be made more or less prominent.

iPad email supports rich text. At this writing, it's the only app included with the iPad that does so. Many third-party apps also support rich text.

iPad email supports the following text effects:

- Bold, italic, and underline
- Indent and "outdent" (reversing the effect of indenting)

Use rich text in iPad email to help you better make your points.

> Having rich text is a plus, but selecting and formatting text is still harder on an iPad than on a computer with a keyboard and a mouse or other pointing device. Keep formatting simple when using your iPad, and consider using a computer for any but the simplest formatting tasks.

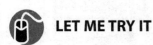 **LET ME TRY IT**

Adding Rich Text to an Email Message

Follow these steps to use text effects in an email message:

1. Create a new email message, or reply to an inbound message.

   The message appears onscreen.

2. Enter text for your message or reply.

3. Select the text that you want to apply text effects to. If you are changing the indentation for a single line of text, you can simply tap to place the cursor in that line of text; the whole line is implicitly selected for indentation purposes.

   The text is displayed as selected.

4. Tap the right arrow in the selection balloon.

   The phrase "Quote Level" appears. If text is selected, the letters **B** / U also appear, as shown in Figure 7.3.

5. To change the quote level, tap Quote Level. Choose Decrease, if the text had previously been indented, or Increase, to indent the text. To add bolding, italic, or underlining, tap the B | U option, then choose Bold, Italics, or Underline.

The text updates to reflect the formatting you've applied.

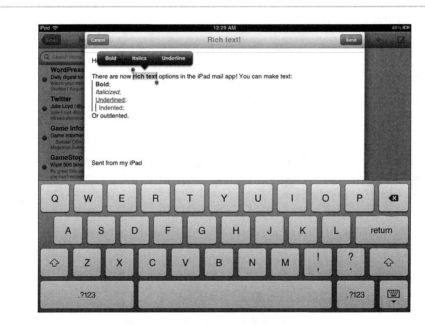

Figure 7.3   *Formatting text helps make things stand out.*

Customizing Your Default Email Signature

Your iPad is set up to include the signature line "Sent from my iPad" at the bottom of each new message you send. This is good advertising for your iPad—and might make you feel cool because you'll be seen to be using such a cool device. It's not that informative for the recipient, however. In fact, they might imagine that you rushed the reply, rather than waiting to send a longer reply from your computer, which would make it easier to type.

Instead, you might want your default email signature to include other information, such as your name, email address, phone number, and so on. That way, even if your email message is forwarded, selectively copied and pasted, and otherwise reused, people who receive the information can easily get back in touch with you.

There are times when you want to use a full, formal email signature, which might include your physical address, Web site or blog, and so on, and other times you might want to use just a couple of lines—perhaps your name, email address, and phone number. I find it useful to have a long email signature that includes everything I might want and then cut out some of the lines when I don't need to include all the information.

Follow these steps to modify your email signature:

1. From the iPad Home screen, tap Settings; then tap Mail > Contacts > Calendars.

2. Tap Signature.

    Your iPad displays the Signature screen, as shown in Figure 7.4.

Figure 7.4   *Update your signature.*

3. To clear the existing signature information, tap the Clear button.

4. Type your custom signature into the text area.

5. When done, press the Mail > Contacts > Calendars button.

You might want to send yourself a test email showing your new signature to get a good idea how it will look to others and to check it for errors.

Receiving and Managing Messages

As you use your iPad, it receives and stores incoming messages. This enables you to keep up with your email even when you're keeping appointments, shopping, or traveling. You can reply to messages, forward messages, save an image or attachment you receive with a message, and delete messages.

The Mail icon on your iPad's Home screen shows the number of unread messages you have at any given time. Keep an eye on this number to see if you've received new messages.

Using your iPad as an email engine is much more fun and easier than using a mobile phone for the same purpose because you can see more of what's going on in your list of messages and within a message. People who had previously taken their laptops on trips find they are can often get by with just the iPad instead. Others carry both, using the laptop for extended work sessions and the iPad for quick email checks, looking things up online, and taking notes in meetings—not to mention watching videos and listening to music.

Checking for New Messages

Keeping up to date on your email messages is a big deal—for some, it might almost be called an obsession. If you have a Wi-Fi-only iPad, you can only receive and send email messages when you have a Wi-Fi connection available. If you have a 3G iPad, you can additionally receive and send email messages when you have a data-capable wireless mobile phone connection, which is likely to be a great deal more of the time.

If you're a Wi-Fi-only iPad user, you can get a device, popularly known as a MiFi, that connects to the mobile phone data network and creates a wireless "bubble" that you can easily connect to with your iPad and laptop. Up to five devices are supported at one time, which might make you quite popular at a business meeting that takes place outside the office. See Chapter 3, "Connecting to the Internet," for more information.

Following are two types of email accounts, which act differently when you check for new messages:

- **Push:** Email services such as MobileMe and Microsoft Exchange support email push, which is very convenient. The server sends, or "pushes," each message to your devices, almost as soon as they're received by the server.

Messages appear in your email Inbox with no specific effort on your part. The iPad has Push turned on by default.

- **Fetch:** Other email services require you to set up your iPad to periodically request new messages, or to manually request the latest and greatest for your Inbox to be brought up to date. This is less handy but saves battery power. You can also turn off push capability on a push-capable service and fetch emails instead to save battery life and to give you more control of how up-to-date you are.

The iPad is rightly celebrated for its very strong battery life: ten hours for most uses—even playing back a movie—and nine hours if you're also using cellular connectivity on a 3G model. (Battery life is just as strong for the iPad 2 as for the original.) However, if you still need to manage your battery charge carefully, consider turning off push capability and switching Fetch to "Manually." You can also turn off wireless networking and/or 3G access except when you are in the act of updating your inbox or surfing the Web. This will help your battery charge last even longer.

 LET ME TRY IT

Configuring Pushing and Fetching

Follow these steps to turn push email on or off and to set up the fetch interval for your device:

1. From the iPad Home screen, tap Settings; then tap Mail > Contacts > Calendars.

2. Tap Fetch New Data.

3. To avoid receiving pushed messages, slide the Push switch to Off.

   You'll still receive messages when you manually request them.

4. To change the Fetch interval, tap the choice you want—15 minutes, 30 minutes, hourly, or manually.

5. To select different approaches for different email accounts, press Advanced; then choose Fetch or Push and, if applicable, the Fetch interval for each email account.

LET ME TRY IT

Manually Fetching New Messages

You might want to manually fetch messages before checking your email, even if you have push email and automatic fetches set up. One of the key features of email is being up-to-date, and manually fetching messages makes sure that you're completely updated. You might also want to turn off push and/or scheduled fetches to save battery power.

Follow these steps to fetch new messages:

1. Start the Mail app. If your iPad is in portrait (vertical) orientation, tap the Inbox button to see your inbox.

   You see the date and time of the last refresh in the bottom of the inbox area.

2. To refresh a single email account, press the Refresh icon in the lower left of your Inbox.

   Your iPad fetches any new messages for that account.

3. To refresh multiple email accounts at once, press the name of your account to bring up the Mailboxes screen. Press the Refresh icon in the lower left of the Mailboxes screen, as shown in Figure 7.5.

   Your iPad fetches any new messages for all your accounts.

Refresh icon

Figure 7.5 *Use the Refresh icon in the Inbox or Mailboxes screen to refresh your email.*

Reading Messages

Use the Mail app to read the messages you've received. You can read messages for a single account or for all accounts.

Saving images embedded in messages is described in the section, "Saving an Email Message to Your Phone," later in this chapter. You can also play audio attachments in many formats by tapping on them. PDF files, word processing files, meeting invitations, and many other files can open in a program that can handle them; tap the attachment to open it.

The Mail app also gathers chains of messages into *conversations*, or groups that begin with an original message and include replies to that message, replies to the replies, and so on. The messages in a conversation are referred to as *threaded*, with each one connected to the next.

The threaded messages are shown as one conversation in your Inbox; when you choose a conversation, the messages in it display, as if the conversation were a folder. You then have to click an individual message to read it in full. You can turn this functionality off in Settings, as described in this section, and deal with email messages individually if you prefer.

Conversations and threading are simpler to understand and manage when the conversation is only between two parties. When more people are involved, and when people are added into or left out of the thread along the way, it can be a lot harder to keep up with a discussion or to find a needed email. The iPad's search capabilities are limited, as described in Chapter 1, "Getting to Know Your iPad"; you could find yourself using another app, such as Gmail, or a computer with a more capable mail client to search for emails that are hard to find using your iPad.

 SHOW ME Media 7.2—Reading Email Messages on Your iPad
Access this video file through your registered Web Edition at
my.safaribooksonline.com/9780132709590/media
or on the DVD for print books.

 LET ME TRY IT

Turning Threading On and Off

By default, your iPad arranges email messages in conversations with threaded messages gathered together. However, you can turn this feature off.

Conversations are convenient for collapsing email messages into chunks of related messages that you can deal with more easily, but conversations also make it harder to find specific email messages—or to spot the connections between different interchanges that occur at the same point in time.

As a result, you might have a strong preference for using or not using conversations and turn the feature on or off for the long term—or you can turn conversations on and off frequently to meet different needs.

Follow these steps to turn threading on and off:

1. From the iPad Home screen, tap Settings; then tap Mail > Contacts > Calendars.

2. Slide the Organize by Thread switch to the opposite position, On or Off.

 LET ME TRY IT

Reading Messages

Unread messages appear with a blue dot next to them. The number of unread messages in an account displays, along with the name of that account.

Follow these steps to read messages:

1. Launch the Mail app. If your iPad is in portrait (vertical) mode, tap the Inbox button to see the Inbox.

   If you want to read messages from the currently selected account, skip to step 4.

2. If you have multiple email accounts and want to change which accounts display in the Inbox, tap the account name or the All Inboxes button in the upper-left corner. If your account supports folders, a list of folders displays; tap Mailbox to see the mailboxes.

   A list of mailboxes displays, as shown in Figure 7.6.

3. To read messages for all your accounts, tap the All Inboxes button. To go straight to the inbox for a specific account, tap the button with the name of that inbox. To go to an account (so you can see the folders in that account), tap the button with the name of that account; then tap Inbox or the folder with the emails you want to see.

   A list of email messages and conversations displays. A conversation with two messages is shown in Figure 7.7.

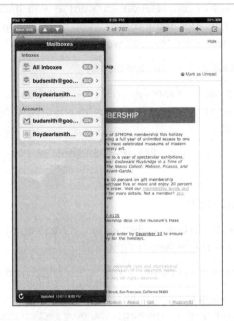

Figure 7.6   *Choose the Inboxes or accounts you want to go to.*

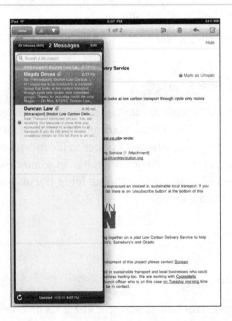

Figure 7.7   *Tap a message to see its contents or tap a conversation to see the messages that make it up.*

4. Tap the message or conversation you want to read. If you tap a conversation, a list of messages in the conversation displays. Tap the message within the conversation that you want to read.

   The email message you selected displays.

5. To zoom in on part of a message, double-tap it. Double-tap again to zoom out. You can also pinch or spread your fingers on the message text to zoom in or out.

6. To see the destination of a link, press and hold it.

   The link's destination address displays.

7. To follow a link, tap it.

   For a Web link, Safari opens, displaying the Web page. For other links, a map or a new email message might open.

8. To mark a message as unread, tap Mark as Unread next to the subject line.

9. To navigate among messages, tap the Next and Previous icons in the upper-right corner of the message. The next section describes other actions you can take.

10. To see more messages, scroll to the bottom of the list of messages and tap the Load More Messages button.

    If you have an active Internet connection, more messages load.

Replying to a Message

You won't always need to reply to messages you receive on your iPad. Also despite the many conveniences of your iPad, you can choose to do the bulk of your email management on a computer, where it's easier to file messages, add, save, or edit attachments, and type long messages or replies. In some cases, you might make a quick reply from your iPad and then a longer reply, possibly with an attachment, from your computer at a later time.

 **LET ME TRY IT**

Replying to a Message

Replying to messages somehow seems to cause a lot of "oh no" moments perhaps because people often do it quickly. Problems with message replies include sending a reply with high emotional content because of being irritated or rushed and using Reply All when there are people on the reply list whom you didn't actually want to include.

The iPad lends itself to replying to email on the go, so think carefully before you reply to avoid making an email etiquette mistake. Follow these steps to reply to a message:

1. In the Mail app, when you see a message you want to reply to, tap it.
   Mail opens the message.

2. Tap the left-pointing arrow in the upper-right corner of your screen, which is the Actions icon.

   Mail displays a list of commands, as shown in Figure 7.8: Reply, Reply All (shown only if there are multiple recipients), Forward, or Print.

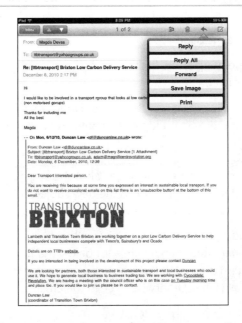

Figure 7.8   *Replying to a message is easy—almost too easy sometimes.*

3. Tap Reply or, if applicable, Reply All.

   The Mail app creates a new message. It has the sender listed in the To: field; any other recipients (if Reply All was selected) listed in the cc: field; the original subject line, with Re: attached to the beginning, as the new subject line; and the original message text added to the bottom of the message.

4. Type your message to the sender. (You also have the opportunity to edit the original message if necessary.)

5. Tap Send.

   The Mail app sends your reply.

Forwarding a Message

Forwarding a message is an important way to keep people up to date and in touch. Here's how to do it on the iPad.

 LET ME TRY IT

Forwarding a Message

1. In the Mail app, when you see a message you want to reply to, tap it to open it.

   Mail opens the message.

2. Tap the left-pointing arrow in the upper-right corner of your screen, which is the Actions icon.

   Mail displays a list of commands (refer to Figure 7.8): Reply, Reply All (shown only if there are multiple recipients), Forward, or Print.

3. Tap Forward.

   The Mail app creates a new message. It has the original subject line with Fwd: attached to the beginning, as the new subject line, and the original message text added to the bottom of the message.

4. In the To: field, type the name and/or email address of the recipients. The contact you want might appear in a list below the To: field; if so, tap to choose it. Alternatively, tap the + button and choose the appropriate contact there, if available. Otherwise, type in the email address.

   The recipient appears in the To: list.

5. Add any additional recipients in the To: list.

6. To enter Cc: and/or Bcc: recipients, tap the Cc:Bcc field; then enter additional recipients—directly in the Cc: or Bcc: area or use the Add button to select from your contacts.

   Remember that other recipients don't see people copied using Bcc, and Bcc recipients are not included in Reply All.

7. Type your message to the sender. (You also have the opportunity to edit the original message if necessary.)

8. Tap Send.

   The Mail app sends your reply.

Saving an Email Image to Your iPad

You can receive photos and other images in email messages. You can easily save a copy of the image to the Photos app on your iPad.

Most images arrive on your iPad by being synchronized to it from your computer, as described in Chapter 10. Although adding images from emails to your iPad is convenient, it does eliminate the exact one-to-one equality between the designated folders on your computer and the contents of the Photos app on your iPad, which can lead to confusion when managing your iPad photos. You might want to add the same image to the designated folders on your computer to keep the contents identical.

 SHOW ME   Media 7.3—Saving an Image from an Email Message
Access this video file through your registered Web Edition at
my.safaribooksonline.com/9780132709590/media
or on the DVD for print books.

 **LET ME TRY IT**

Saving an Email Image to Your iPad

1. In the Mail app, tap the message that contains an image you want to save.

    Mail opens the message.

2. Tap and hold the image.

    The Mail app displays a list of commands (refer to Figure 7.8).

3. Choose Save Image.

    The image is saved in the Photos app.

ⓖ *To learn how to view photos on your iPad, see "Viewing Photos" in Chapter 15.*

Deleting and Moving Messages

You can delete a single message, delete multiple messages, or move messages to a different folder.

LET ME TRY IT

Deleting a Message

1. In the Mail app, open the message that you want to delete.

    Mail opens the message.

2. Tap the Trash Can icon in the upper-right corner.

    The Delete Message button appears.

3. Tap the Delete Message button.

    The message is deleted.

 LET ME TRY IT

Moving a Message

1. In the Mail app, open the message that you want to move.

    Mail opens the message.

2. Tap the folder icon in the upper-right corner.

    A list of folders for the current account appears.

3. Navigate to the destination account and folder you desire and tap it.

    The message is moved.

 LET ME TRY IT

Deleting or Moving Multiple Messages

1. In the Mail app, in a list of messages, tap the Edit button.

    Open circles appear next to the email messages.

2. Tap next to each message that you want to delete or move.

    A check mark appears next to each selected message, as shown in Figure 7.9.

Figure 7.9   *Selected messages appear checked.*

3. To delete the messages, click the button with the trash can icon or the word Delete at the bottom of the list of messages.

The messages are deleted.

4. To move the images, click the button with a folder and the word Move at the bottom of the list of messages.

A list of folders appears.

5. Tap the folder you want to move the images to.

The images are moved to the selected folder.

6. To avoid deleting or moving the files, press the Cancel button at the top of the list of messages.

The messages are not deleted or moved.

In this chapter you learn how to synchronize, create, and manage contacts using the Contacts app.

8

Managing Contacts on Your iPad

As you go about your day, you meet new people all the time—and learn new things about people you already know. And you need to reach out, get in touch, or act on some partly remembered detail. The iPad's Contacts app makes this easy.

The large screen of the iPad makes it quicker to search for a person, scroll through a list of names, or find a phone number or other important piece of information. The iPad is also easy to use for entering new information quickly and conveniently.

Depending on how you set up your email accounts, your contact information may be synchronized with another source based on an email account—whether that's an Apple mail account, a Microsoft Exchange server, or a webmail application. This makes your iPad into a portable terminal for contacts and related information, such as email and calendaring.

The easiest way to synchronize your contacts is to set up synchronization for email and include contacts among the items that are synchronized along with email messages. To learn more about synchronizing contact information along with email messages, see Chapter 6, "Setting Up Email."

You maintain your contact information through the Contacts app. It's shown in Figure 8.1. It's quite similar to an old-fashioned address book, with indented tabs for each letter. The letters are so close together that it's hard to tap the right one. So the easiest way to get to a specific letter is to run a finger or thumb up and down along the tabs, watching them change.

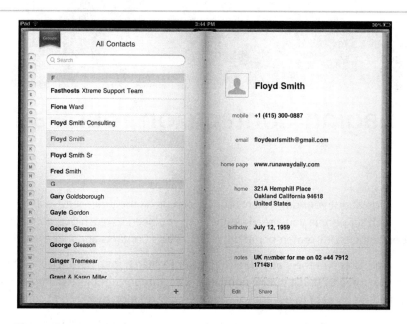

Figure 8.1 *Drag your finger up and down the letters to get the one you want.*

The Contacts app takes better advantage of the available screen space, and uses a slightly larger font, when you use it in landscape mode (holding the iPad horizontally) rather than portrait mode.

Keeping your contact information up to date makes it easier to use email, calendaring, and other tools as well. For example, in email, you can start to type in someone's actual name; their name and email address appear in a scrolling list that you can pick the right contact from. Similarly, you can tap a person's address, and it appears in the Maps app, drawing from information in your Contacts. From there, you can easily get directions to or from the location.

You may find performance problems with large contacts lists with a smartphone or with the iPad. Usability for large lists is also better on a computer than it is on an iPad, let alone on a smartphone.

Some people have thousands of contacts, either in their regular contacts list, or in specific places such as LinkedIn. You may need to keep the list of contacts that you sync in the hundreds, rather than the thousands, to get acceptable performance and usability on your smartphone and iPad as well as on a computer.

Take advantage of the iPad's capabilities to stay on top of, and interact with, the latest information about friends, family, and professional connections.

Synchronizing Contacts

You may have two different sets of contacts: work contacts, which may well be maintained on Microsoft Exchange or Lotus Notes, and personal contacts. Or you may have them all integrated into one big list. It may even be that you'll create your first online list of contacts now, on your iPad.

In most cases, you want to synchronize your iPad contacts with contacts on other devices. You have several choices:

- **Mac OS X:** Use the Address Book application on your Mac.

- **Windows:** Use Outlook or the Windows Contacts app.

- **Microsoft Exchange:** You may have contacts on an Exchange server, usually at work, with which you want to synchronize.

- **Online:** You can use Google contacts or Yahoo! contacts. Online contacts are more likely to update seamlessly and automatically, without any effort on your part. This way, you don't have to explicitly synchronize your iPad to your computer to get updated information from one to the other.

If you don't yet use any of these, consider moving to one of them, particularly one of the online choices, if possible. By staying in sync, you can have seamless access to contacts across your computer and, with some additional effort, your mobile phone.

You can set up or manage synchronization of contacts using iTunes.

 LET ME TRY IT

Synchronizing Contacts

1. Connect your iPad to your Macintosh or Windows PC. Your iPad appears in the Devices list in iTunes.

2. Click your iPad in the Devices branch. iTunes displays the Summary tab.

3. Click the Info tab. Synchronization information appears.

4. On Windows, click the Sync Contacts With check box to activate it; then use the list to choose your Windows contacts program, such as Outlook. The result is shown in Figure 8.2. On a Mac, activate the Sync Address Book Contacts check box.

5. To sync your entire address book to your iPad, choose All Contacts. To sync selected groups online, choose Selected Groups; then activate the check box for each group you want to include in synchronization.

Figure 8.2   *On Windows, check the Sync Contacts With check box.*

6. You can choose whether contacts created on your iPad outside of the selected groups are synced to your overall list of contacts. Check the check box with a long name: Add Contacts Created Outside of Groups on This iPad To. Then, from the menu, choose the group you want the contacts to sync to.

7. On a Mac, to sync either Yahoo! Address Book contacts or Google Contacts, check the appropriate box. Then, when prompted, enter your Yahoo! or Google user name and password.

8. Click Apply. iTunes synchronizes contacts between your computer and your iPad.

9. When the sync is complete, to end the synchronization session, click the Eject icon next to the name of your iPad in the iTunes Device list.

Creating a New Contact

Synchronizing contacts, either by direct connection or through cloud services such as Apple, Google, or Yahoo!, is a great way to populate your contacts list on your iPad. Synchronizing can also keep your contacts list refreshed with new contacts that come in from other devices you use.

However, your iPad is also great for picking up new contact information while you're out and about. The ease of using the iPad, with its large screen, makes getting contact information into the iPad easier. And with ongoing synchronization, the contact information you gather on the iPad can show up on your other devices as well. Your iPad time can thus contribute to your ease and comfort even when you're using a computer or a mobile phone.

Entering a lot of information through the touchscreen can be a bit of work, so in this chapter, the task is divided into different sections for each type of information. (And hopefully, dividing the task helped you to conquer it.) All sections use the Add Contact screen (refer to Figure 8.1). To reach this screen, open the Contacts app, and then tap the Add icon (+) to open the New Contact screen.

There's no one best way to orient your iPad while entering a contact. Holding the iPad in portrait (vertical) mode, as shown in Figure 8.3, gives you a small keyboard, but an overview of all fields available for contact information. Holding the iPad in landscape (horizontal) mode, as shown in Figure 8.4, gives you a bigger onscreen keyboard, but only a few of the contact fields at a time.

Figure 8.3   *In portrait mode, you can see all the Contact fields.*

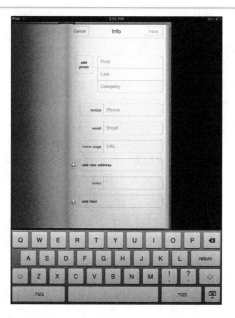

Figure 8.4 *In landscape mode, you have access to a big keyboard for typing Contact info.*

These steps show you how to start a new contact.

 LET ME TRY IT

Starting a New Contact

1. On the Home screen, tap the Contacts icon. Your iPad launches the Contacts app.

> The iPad version of the Contacts app has read-only support for the Groups capability in Google contacts, among others. Tap the Groups ribbon to see groups for your contacts and to choose a contact from a group for viewing or editing. You cannot, however, put contacts into groups from within the iPad Contacts app.

2. Tap inside the First field, and type the contact's first name. If your contact has a middle name that you want to include, enter it after the first name. (Same for multiple middle names.) For a company entry, leave this field blank.

3. Tap inside the Last field, and type the contact's last name. For a company entry, leave this field blank.

4. Tap inside the Company field, and type the company name. If you enter a company, leave the First and Last fields blank, and enter this field only.

Adding a Phone Number

The phone field starts with a default value of "mobile" for the type of phone number. Don't worry if the number you have is not a mobile number; you'll have an opportunity to change this designation after you enter the actual phone number. These steps show you how to add a phone number to a contact.

 LET ME TRY IT

Adding a Phone Number to a Contact

1. Tap the Phone field.

> The iPad version of the Contacts app doesn't support Groups for Google contacts, among others. You may have to manage this, and possibly other fields, in the version of the service that's available as a personal computer program or via a Web browser.

2. Type the contact's phone number, or paste it in. You can use a variety of formats, including parentheses around the area code, dashes or no dashes, and so on. The iPad formats the number to its standards. For numbers that require a pause, such as some office extensions, insert a comma for a pause of about 1 second.

   As you enter the number, a new field opens up for an additional phone number. The label is different than the label for the current phone number; for instance, if you already specified that you entered a number with the Mobile label, the Contacts app may label the next one Home.

3. Tap the label to the left of the phone number. The default label for the first phone number you enter is Mobile. The Contacts app displays the Label screen, as shown in Figure 8.5. It lists the labels you can assign to the phone number.

4. To add additional phone numbers, repeat steps 1 through 3 for additional phone numbers. Capture all the phone numbers you can get a hold of at any given point; this gives you much more flexibility to reach out to people later.

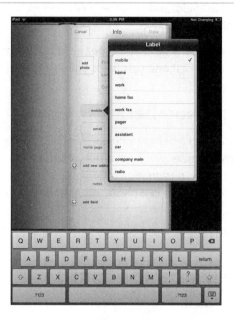

Figure 8.5   *You have lots of choices for the type of phone number.*

    SHOW ME   Media 8.1—Understanding the Usefulness of
Contact Labels

Access this video file through your registered Web Edition at
my.safaribooksonline.com/9780132709590/media
or on the DVD for print books.

Adding an Email Address

Note that the email address starts with a default value of "home" for the type of
email address. (I've found that it might better be labeled "personal" because people
enter their personal email addresses from all sorts of places.) Don't worry if the
email address you have is not a home (or personal) email address; you'll have an
opportunity to change this designation after you enter the actual email address.

Following are the steps to add an email address to a contact.

LET ME TRY IT

Adding an Email Address to a Contact

1. Tap the Email field.

2. Type the contact's email address, or paste it in from another source, such as an email message. As you begin to enter the email address, another field opens up for you to type an additional email address.

3. If you want to add an additional email address, repeat steps 1 and 2. Capture all the email addresses you can; this gives you more flexibility to reach out to people later.

Adding a Home Page Address

You can add the address of a person's Web home page to a contact. This can also be a Facebook page address, Skype designation, or something similar. You can enter multiple Web addresses; as you enter one, a new field opens up for another.

If your contact works at an organization and has a personal home page, you may want to include the personal home page in the person's contact. Then create a separate contact for the person's organization, and enter the organizational home page there. Use the Notes field, described in a later section, to tie them together, to refer to one record from the other.

Follow these steps to add a home page address to a contact.

LET ME TRY IT

Adding a Home Page Address to a Contact

1. Tap the Home page field.

2. Type the contact's Web address, or paste it in. As you begin to enter the home page address, another field opens up for you to type an additional Web address.

3. If you want to add an additional Web address, repeat steps 1 and 2. As with other information, enter all the Web addresses you can; this gives you more flexibility in reaching out to people later.

Adding a Street Address

In these Internet-oriented times, it can seem like unnecessary work to capture a street address. However, there are times when the address can be valuable. The address is especially useful if you need to use the Maps app to get to, or near, the address as a destination—or if you want to send a holiday card or birthday card.

Following are the steps to add a street address to a contact.

 LET ME TRY IT

Adding a Street Address to a Contact

1. Tap the Plus symbol next to the Add New Address field, or tap directly in the Add New Address field.

   The address area opens up: Street, City, State, ZIP, and Country.

2. The type of address defaults to a home address. To change it, tap the word Home. Choices appear: Work and Other. Choose the appropriate label.

3. Tap the Street field, and enter the contact's street address.

   An additional Street field opens up, in case there is additional information for the address. Enter this information, if available.

   The Maps app uses the address to plot the location of the contact. Be careful, though, about adding information that the Maps app might not understand, such as the floor of a building that a business or a personal contact is on; it might confuse the app. Consider entering such information in the Notes area instead.

4. If there's additional addressing information, tap the second Street field and enter the remainder of the contact's street address.

5. Tap the City field, and enter the city name.

6. Tap the State field, and enter the state or province. For clarity, in the United States, use the official two-letter state code, which you can find online at the United States Postal Service website: http://www.usps.com/ncsc/lookups/usps_abbreviations.html.

7. Tap the ZIP field, and enter the ZIP code or postal code for the contact. You can find both the five-digit ZIP code for an address—and, even better, the ZIP+4 code—online, at the United States Postal Service's ZIP4 website: http://zip4.usps.com/zip4/.

Handwritten ZIP codes and ZIP+4 codes are often machine-readable, which speeds the delivery of your mail. A ZIP+4 code is specific enough to enable machine sorting of your mail right to specific letter carrier, saving a big step (and potentially getting your mail to its destination a day earlier). So it's useful to have this information in your Contacts.

8. The country name defaults to your home country. To change it, tap the country name; then choose the country name from the scrolling list, as shown in Figure 8.6.

Figure 8.6 *Finding your country in the regional lists can be a bit tough.*

The country names are grouped by continent or major region, which can be confusing compared to a straight alphabetical list. To help you navigate through the list, the regions, in the order in which they appear in the list, are: Africa (Eastern, Middle, Northern, Southern, and Western); America (Central, North, and South); Asia (Central, Eastern, South-Eastern, Southern, Western); Caribbean; Europe; and Oceania. It's often difficult to guess which region a country in, say, the middle area of Africa is.

9. As you finish, a new address area opens up. To add another address, repeat steps 1 through 8; enter the type of address, street, city, state, ZIP code, and country.

Your choice of type of address is limited—if you've already entered a Home address, for instance, your choices are limited to Work and Other. That is, you can't enter two home addresses, for example.

When you have a second address up, to change the designation of the first address you entered, you have to change the second address to the value you don't want to use, change the first address to the needed value, and then change the second address to its needed value.

 SHOW ME   Media 8.2—Assigning a Photo to a Contact
Access this video file through your registered Web Edition at
my.safaribooksonline.com/9780132709590/media
or on the DVD for print books.

Adding a Photo

Facebook and other applications have made people very much used to seeing photos next to information from specific people. Some applications find photos automatically, so you don't have to do anything (unless you don't like your automatically chosen photo); others enable you to manage it. WordPress blogging software and many other online services use something called a Gravatar, which is a central point for managing your photo or other image to be used across many applications.

On the iPad, though, the process to assign a photo is explicit. After you assign a photo, though, it can be used on your iPhone and Mac, if you have them, and perhaps elsewhere as well.

The iPad enables you to zoom in on part of an existing photo and use the zoomed-in portion as the contact photo.

Follow these steps to enter your photo.

 LET ME TRY IT

Adding a Photo to a Contact

1. If it's not already available, bring the photo you want to use into your iPad. To learn how to do it, see Chapter 15, "Importing and Viewing Photos."

2. At the top of the New Contact screen, tap Add Photo. A list of available photo albums appears.

3. Tap to choose a photo album. Thumbnails of photos appear.

4. Tap to choose a photo. The photo appears in the Move and Scale screen, as shown in Figure 8.7.

Figure 8.7   *When you tap the photo you want for your contact, use the Move and Scale screen to pan to and zoom in on the portion of the image that you want to use.*

5. To zoom in, put two fingertips next to each other on the screen; then spread them apart.

6. To zoom back out, put two fingertips spread apart on the screen; then pinch them together.

7. To pan, put a single fingertip on the screen and move it (and the image) around. The image used for your contact is quite small. Therefore, it's best to zoom in quite closely on the person's face if you want to recognize it. (Though you might recognize the person from a distinctive position or background as well.)

8. When you're happy with the image, tap Use. The Contacts app assigns the photo to the contact.

Adding Notes to a Contact

You might often find that you have information associated with a contact that doesn't actually fit in any of the fields you have. Sometimes, the information is an annotation to existing fields—for instance, you might have noted the hours a friend is usually home next to the address.

In the past, this kind of information would have been a marginal note in your address book, next to the address itself. However, in your Contact information, you can only put the address itself—or you can't use the address to drive the Maps application and get directions to the person's house. (This type of problem also comes up when making appointments, as described in the next chapter.)

You can put this additional information, and other comments about the contact, in the Notes field. Get in the habit of adding this kind of extra data whenever you have it. Then, get in the habit of checking your contacts for notes before using them; otherwise, you might miss this kind of valuable additional information.

To add a Note to a contact, simply tap in the Notes field, and type the additional information. You can also type it in another app, such as the Notes app, and copy and paste it into the Notes field.

The Notes area of a contact holds hundreds of characters. However, such a small area displays that it's hard to use more than a few lines worth of information, as you can see from Figure 8.8. The most you could fit into the Notes area displayed in the Contacts app on your iPad is approximately 250 characters, or approximately 40 words.

Figure 8.8   *The Notes field is useful for small chunks of information.*

Adding Additional Fields

The iPad Contacts app enables you to add additional fields to a contact, choosing from 11 available fields:

- **Prefix:** Useful for distinguishing a Miss from a Ms. from a Mrs., adding the Dr. prefix for those with the appropriate qualifications, and so on.

- **Phonetic first name:** Sometimes you need a reminder of how to say a first name. For instance, I have a friend, Luis, who is "Lewis" to some friends and "Loo-ees" to others. You can add that kind of reminder for yourself here.

- **Phonetic last name:** Just as some first names need pronunciation reminders, so do some last names. Enter that here.

- **Middle:** There's no room for middle names or initials in the fields provided by default, but this can be valuable information. For instance, because my name is Bud E. Smith, to distinguish me from a few other Bud Smiths out there, I like having room for the middle initial.

- **Suffix:** You can specify whether someone is a Jr. or Sr., add an academic qualification such as an MBA, or add professional certifications here.

- **Nickname:** Again, very useful, if only to help you remember that your company's new CEO was known as "Poochie" in her college days.

- **Job Title:** Useful for all sorts of contacts.

- **Department:** In big companies in particular, having the department a person works in can be a big deal. ("Do you mean the Bud Smith in accounting, the one in sales, or ...?")

- **Twitter:** The contact's Twitter handle. Apple may increase the integration of its products with Twitter over time, so start capturing Twitter handles or your contacts wherever possible.

- **Profile:** The contact's social media contact name; choose from among Facebook (the default), Flickr, LinkedIn, Myspace, or a custom service. For a custom service, you type the name of the service as the field name, and then the contact's name on that service.

- **Instant message:** Enter an IM address. This field enables you to change the label among AIM, Yahoo! Messenger, MSN Messenger, ICQ, and Jabber. (For a Skype or similar address not listed here, use the Notes field so that you can label it properly.)

- **Birthday:** A great thing to be reminded of when it rolls around.

- **Date:** When you tap this, you're asked to enter a date under the heading, Anniversary. You can use it to enter other dates, too. For bonus points, make a note as to what the date is for in the Note field.

- **Related People:** Add the names of relatives—mother (the default), father, parent, brother, sister, child, friend, spouse, partner, assistant, manager, other, or a custom label. For a custom label, you type the label name, then the field. Perfect for today's complicated family situations!

Follow these steps to use the Add Field area.

 LET ME TRY IT

Adding Other Fields to a Contact

1. Tap in the Add Field area, or the + symbol next to it. The Contacts app displays the Add Field screen with the extra fields just described: name-related fields Prefix, Phonetic First Name, Phonetic Last Name, Middle, Suffix, and Nickname; jobs-related fields Job Title and Department; and Instant Message, Birthday, and Date.

2. Tap the field you want to add. The field appears in the relevant part of the Add Contact screen; for instance, if you tap Middle, the Middle field appears between First (name) and Last (name).

3. Tap in the new field, and enter the data for it.

4. For the IM field, tap the service name AIM to choose from among AIM, Yahoo! Messenger, MSN Messenger, ICQ, and Jabber.

5. To add additional fields, repeat steps 1 through 4 for each field.

Completing the New Contact

After you populate all the existing fields, create notes, and add those fields you deem relevant, it's time to complete the contact.

Follow these steps to complete the new contact.

 LET ME TRY IT

Completing the New Contact

1. Check the data you've entered carefully. If the data is accurate, and formatted correctly, you can reuse it for many purposes. For instance, you can use address information in the Maps app on the iPad, and you can use phone number information to complete calls from a mobile phone.

2. Tap the Done button at the top of the screen to save the information or Cancel to delete it. You return to the All Contacts screen.

Editing a Contact

You can get contact information into your iPad in a number of ways—by syncing via a physical connection to your computer, by having information pushed over the Internet, and by creating contacts yourself.

The real art of having useful contacts, however, is to keep correcting, updating, and adding to them as you pick up new information. This way, your iPad and other electronic systems become a truly useful support system. Your iPad can be a bit like the royal aide who whispers guest's names in the monarch's ear at a diplomatic function!

These steps allow you to edit a contact.

SHOW ME   Media 8.3—Creating a Contact
Access this video file through your registered Web Edition at
my.safaribooksonline.com/9780132709590/media
or on the DVD for print books.

LET ME TRY IT

Editing a Contact

1. On the Home screen, tap the Contacts icon. Your iPad launches the Contacts app.

2. Use the alphabetical tabs on the left to move quickly to your contact. Or if it's enabled for your contacts, use the Groups ribbon.

3. Tap the Contact you want to edit; then tap the Edit button.

   The Contacts app opens on the Info screen, as shown in Figure 8.9

Figure 8.9   *Display the contact you want; then tap Edit to open it for editing.*

4. To change existing data, tap the data inside the field. Tap the X button that appears to clear the field, or edit the contents.

5. To add data in an empty field, tap inside the field and type the new data.

6. To remove a field, tap the red Delete icon to the left of the field; then tap the Delete button that appears.

7. To add a new field, see Adding Other Fields to a Contact in the previous section.

8. Tap the Done button at the top of the screen to save the information, or Cancel to delete it. You return to the All Contacts screen, with the contact you just edited selected and highlighted.

Deleting a Contact

Getting rid of contacts makes it easier to navigate your contacts list, shortens the list of names that appears when you enter an email address in the Mail list, and so on. So consider deleting contacts when you can.

You may find it useful to save the information in a contact somewhere that isn't in the Contacts list but is still accessible—such as a spreadsheet or word processing file. Unfortunately, there's no easy way to do this on the iPad. However, you may want to periodically export your contacts information to another type of file on your computer, if possible.

These steps allow you to delete a contact.

 LET ME TRY IT

Deleting a Contact

1. On the Home screen, tap the Contacts icon. Your iPad launches the Contacts app.

2. Use the alphabetical tabs on the left to move quickly to the contact you want to remove. Or if it's enabled for your contacts, use the Groups ribbon.

3. Tap the Contact you want to edit; then tap the Edit button. The Contacts app opens on the Info screen for that contact.

4. Tap the Delete Contact button at the bottom of the Info screen. (You may have to scroll down to see it.) The Contacts app displays a dialog asking you to delete the contact, or cancel the operation, as shown in Figure 8.10.

5. Tap Delete to remove the contact. The Contacts app removes the contact. There is no Undo function for deleted contacts.

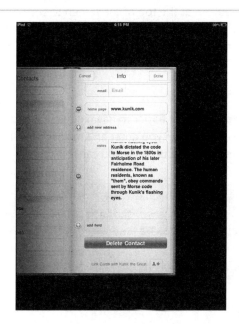

Figure 8.10   *In today's world, it's deleting that's such sweet sorrow.*

In this chapter you learn how to synchronize your calendar, navigate the calendar, add and edit events, read and respond to invitations via Exchange, and follow another person's calendar.

9

Tracking Appointments and Events

The iPad's capability to track appointments and remind you of where you're supposed to be, and when, is one of its more powerful capabilities. It's great to store lots of information for a specific appointment and also zoom out to manage your calendar a week or a month at a time.

With synchronization, your calendar is tied into calendar functions on other devices, such as your mobile phone and the computers you use. Your iPad becomes a viewer of your calendar and a tool to update a calendar that you can also access from a personal computer and a mobile phone. The iPad has a special role among these tools, combining strong portability with excellent usability, both for viewing and adding calendar events. The more you learn to use the calendar functions on your iPad, the better you can keep your calendar up to date, and your life organized and easier.

 TELL ME MORE   Media 9.1—The iPad Calendar Versus Other Calendars

Access this audio recording through your registered Web Edition at
my.safaribooksonline.com/9780132709590/media
or on the DVD for print books.

Synchronizing Calendar Information

One of the most important functions for a calendar is to remind you of appointments. So you want your appointments to show up on your iPad, even if you initially enter them on a phone or computer, and vice versa. Synchronization loads your iPad calendar with appointments when you first set it up and keeps the calendar information on your iPad and your other devices aligned as you use them.

As with contacts, the easiest way to synchronize your calendar information is to set up synchronization for email and include calendar entries among the items synchronized along with email messages.

⊙ *To learn more about synchronizing contact and calendar information along with email messages, see Chapter 6, "Setting Up Email."*

As with contacts, described in the previous chapter, you can synchronize calendar information to the Mac OS X Address Book, to Outlook on Windows, to Microsoft Exchange, or to cloud-based services such as the Google calendar or Yahoo! calendar. If you don't yet use any of these, you can adopt one of them to help connect your iPad calendar to your other devices. You can also set up or manage synchronization of your calendar using iTunes. The steps below show the process using iTunes, as it's the approach that works for all users.

 LET ME TRY IT

Synchronizing Calendars

1. Connect your iPad to your Macintosh or Windows PC. Your iPad appears in the Devices list in iTunes.

2. Click your iPad in the Devices branch. iTunes displays the Summary tab.

3. Click the Info tab. Synchronization information appears.

4. On Windows, click the Sync Calendars With check box to activate it; then use the list to choose your Windows contacts program, for instance Outlook. This is almost identical to the Sync Contacts With screen shown in the previous chapter, in Figure 8.2. On a Mac, activate the Sync iCal Calendars check box.

5. To sync all your events to the iPad, leave the All Calendars radio button selected. To sync only the events from some calendars, choose the Selected Calendars radio button; then click the check box beside each calendar you want to synchronize with to activate it.

6. To set a limit on the time frame for synchronization, click the check box next to the setting. Do not sync events older than 30 days to activate it. Then change the number of days from the default, 30, to the value that makes sense to you in your circumstances.

   You might find that you rarely change old calendar entries and therefore don't need to synchronize far back into the past.

7. Click Apply. iTunes synchronizes your computer's calendars to your iPad. If you add new calendar events on your iPad, or change or delete events, those changes are synced to your computer as well.

8. When the sync completes, to end the synchronization session, click the Eject icon next to the name of your iPad in the iTunes Device list.

Figure out and maintain a reliable plan to keep your calendars synchronized. This can help you avoid problems with having different information in different places so that you get the most out of your iPad.

 SHOW ME Media 9.2—Navigating Your Calendar
Access this video file through your registered Web Edition at
my.safaribooksonline.com/9780132709590/media
or on the DVD for print books.

Navigating the Calendar

Use the Calendar app to work with calendars on your iPad. Figure 9.1 shows the Month view, one of the many Calendar screens.

Figure 9.1 *Tap the Calendar icon to open the Calendar app and view your schedule and to add, change, or delete entries.*

The Week view shows off the iPad's usefulness with the Calendar to the device's best advantage. The large viewing area makes a big (no pun intended) difference. Entries are quite readable. You can even rotate the iPad between landscape (horizontal) and portrait (vertical) modes to emphasize breadth (across the week) versus depth (for each day) in how you look at your week's calendar entries.

Following are five different views available for you to use with the Calendar app:

- **Day:** If you need to take things one day at a time, the Calendar app can help. The iPad screen has so much space available that the Calendar gives you both a list of events and an hourly view of your day, as shown in Figure 9.2.

Figure 9.2 *The Day view gives you a couple of different ways to look at your day.*

- **Week:** This is my favorite view in the Calendar. Using the iPad's large screen, it effectively relates today's activities to those in the surrounding week.

- **Month:** If you have a lot going on, the Month view shows only about a dozen characters per entry; it can be a bit dense and hard to make sense of. Use the Month view, as shown in Figure 9.3, to get an overview of your activities and then the Week or Day view to get more details.

- **Year:** The year view, shown in Figure 9.4, is a kind of "heat map" of your busy (red), somewhat busy (orange), lightly busy (yellow), and non-busy (white) days. It's most useful as a way to move around from one month to a different month by leaps and bounds. You won't find a Year view on other iOS devices—the iPhone and iPod touch.

Figure 9.3   *The Month view is best used for a quick overview.*

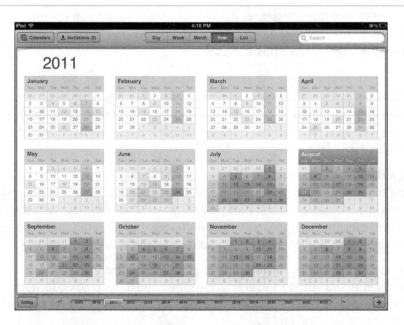

Figure 9.4   *The Year view is a "heat map" of your busy-ness.*

- **List:** The List view, shown in Figure 9.5, is almost identical to the Day view, but the list on the left side of the screen extends indefinitely into the future, rather than being confined to the current day. Sometimes useful, but not a view where you're likely to spend a lot of time.

Figure 9.5   *The List view is flexible and scrollable.*

To navigate in any view, use the arrow keys at the bottom, near the corners, to move one day, week, or month backward or forward at a time. (The List view works like the Day view.) You can also press on a specific day, week, or month, as shown at the bottom of the screen.

Unlike specific weeks or months, individual days in the Day view are packed in so close together at the bottom of the page that it's difficult to tap the right one on the first try. Instead, press and hold near the specific day that you want; then drag. Use the highlight that appears above your finger—showing the day you're pressing—as a guide, and drag left or right as needed to get to the correct day.

To move farther and faster, drag your finger quickly across the list of days at the bottom of the screen. Hold your finger at either end to keep going forward or backward in time, beyond the currently displayed set of days, weeks, or months.

In the List view, to see the list for previous or future days, just drag the list up or down indefinitely.

Adding Events to the Calendar

If you synchronize calendars frequently, you might find that many of your calendar entries are most easily added from a personal computer. Some of the entry steps for calendars are easier using a mouse and physical keyboard rather than the iPad's touchscreen and onscreen keyboard. Grabbing event information from an email or Facebook page, for instance, and pasting it into the fields of a calendar entry is easier to do on a computer.

However, the iPad has the tremendous advantages of great portability and convenience. You might have your iPad handy at times when you don't have a personal computer nearby. You might even carry your computer less and less, and your iPad more and more.

As you carry your iPad more, you may often find it convenient to add events on-the-go onto your iPad Calendar, as describe here. You can then sync them later, or they may sync automatically via a cloud-based service such as Google Mail or Yahoo! Mail.

You can specify a number of features for an event: the date, start and end time, location, repetition (if any), invitees, alert, and availability indicator.

Adding Core Information for an Event

Core information for an event is "just the facts," meaning the event name and when and where it occurs. For many events, this is all you need. Also, if you're in a hurry, you may want to enter only core information and then enter additional information later.

Follow these steps to add core information for an event.

 LET ME TRY IT

Adding Core Information for an Event

1. From the iPad Home screen, tap the Calendar app to open it.

2. Navigate to the date you want. If you are in Week or Month view, the date of the event defaults to the current date. If you tap within the area of a different date, the date of the event initially sets to the date you tap.

3. Tap the Add (+) icon. The Calendar app displays the Add Event screen, as shown in Figure 9.6. The cursor displays in the Title area of the Add Event screen, and the keyboard appears onscreen as well.

Figure 9.6   *A new event is set to occur on the current date or the one you tapped in most recently.*

4. Enter the event title. As you enter the title, be aware that in many views of calendar events, only the first ten or so characters of the event title display. So front-load the event title that you enter with distinguishing information, such as the name of the person you're meeting. Leave out superfluous words such as "meeting."

5. Tap the Location box and enter the event location. Enter the Location in a format that Google Maps can understand, so you can use Google Maps to help you get to the location. If you have additional information that's unlikely to be understood by Google Maps, such as "fourth floor" or "near the market" or "red building," consider including this information in the Notes, or even in the event title, if you want to be sure to see it.

6. Tap the Starts/Ends box to enter the event starting and ending times. The Calendar app displays the Start & End screen, as shown in Figure 9.7. The Starts area is highlighted.

7. Use the time wheel to set the event's starting time. Be sure to set the AM/PM designator correctly. The ending time adjusts to 1 hour later than the starting time.

Figure 9.7 *Set the event starting and ending times.*

8. If needed, use the time wheel to change the event's ending time.

> Don't include driving or other transport times in your meeting time; it might confuse you, or other people you invite, about when the event actually starts. Block off these chunks of time as separate events, even if it seems like a hassle to enter multiple events.

9. Use the All-Day slider to indicate whether an event takes the whole day.

> An all-day event displays as a small indicator at the top of your calendar screen. It doesn't actually block off the time on your calendar, making it easy to accidentally double-book times during that day. This makes the All-Day event option good for reminders, such as birthdays, but not so good for events such as all-day meetings. Consider entering events that have specific start and end times using those times, even if the event is quite extensive, rather than as all-day events. Or enter such events both as all-day events and as specific, time-limited events.

10. Tap Done to complete the entry of the event start and end times. You return to the Add Event screen. This completes the core information for an event.

11. If you finish entering information for the event, tap Done; the event closes and is added to the calendar. Otherwise, leave the event open to see the next set of steps to complete entering information.

SHOW ME   Media 9.3—Setting Up a Repeating Event
Access this video file through your registered Web Edition at
my.safaribooksonline.com/9780132709590/media
or on the DVD for print books.

Editing and Adding Information for an Event

Additional information for an event goes beyond "just the facts" and enables you to specify whether the event repeats, who's invited, what alert you want to set to remind you of the event, your availability, and to add any notes. This is information that you might add at the time that you create an event, or you might come back to a previously created event and add this later.

Follow these steps to add additional information for an event.

LET ME TRY IT

Editing and Adding Information for an Event

1. If the event isn't open, navigate to it and tap the event to open it. Make any needed changes in the title, location, and start and end times. If the event is already open, continue with the next step.

2. To enter repetition, tap the Repeat box. In the Repeat Event screen that appears, choose a frequency of repetition: Every Day, Every Week, Every 2 Weeks, Every Month, or Every Year.

    The options here are not as robust as on some other platforms. For instance, you can't specify repetition by day of the month (that is, the fourth Thursday of the month), only by the specific date of the month. You may want to use another platform to access a broader range of specifications.

> If you synchronize your calendar with other devices, either by connection to your computer or via the cloud, you may want to use another device, which displays more options, to create or edit the event; the event then shows up properly on your iPad. For Gmail, for instance, you can use the Safari browser on your iPad to access your calendar and set the repetition options there.

3. To begin inviting people, tap the Invitees box. The Add Invitees screen opens.

4. To continue inviting people, tap the Add (+) symbol in the Invitees box. From the list of contacts that appears (see Figure 9.8), type part of a name to home in on it; the list of matches updates with each character you type. Alternatively, scroll the list up and down by dragging your finger, or tap a letter in the list to the right.

Only parts of a name that match the beginning or end of a name are matched; characters within a name, such as "mit" in "Smith," won't be. (So searching for "mit" would bring up "Mitchell," but not "Smith.")

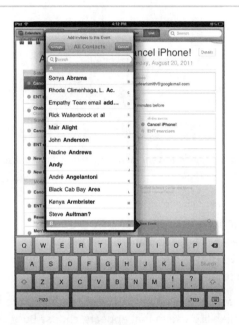

Figure 9.8 *Add people to invite to your event.*

5. To invite people from additional lists, tap the Groups button. From the Groups screen that opens, choose other lists and select people from those as well. Click Cancel to return to the Add Invitees screen.

You can't enter an email address or other contact information directly from here. Consider entering a new contact, as described in the previous chapter, or using a different platform to invite people.

6. Click Done to finish inviting people. You return to the Add Event screen.

7. To set an alert for the meeting, tap Alert. The Event Alert screen appears, as shown in Figure 9.9.

Figure 9.9 *Tap Alert to open the Event Alert screen, and then choose how far before the start time you want to be alerted.*

8. To finish setting the alert, tap to choose the amount of time beforehand at which the alert will appear: None, 5 minutes before, 15 minutes, 30 minutes, 1 hour, 2 hours, 1 day, 2 days, or the day of the event. Tap Done when finished. You return to the Add Event screen.

9. To specify how your availability will be shown to others, tap Availability. From the Availability screen that appears, choose Busy, Free, Tentative, or Out of Office. Click Done to finish specifying your availability.

    The specifics of how your availability displays to people depends on what platform they use to view your calendar information.

10. To enter a note, tap in the Notes area. Type your note. Notes can include additional address information, suggestions as to transportation time, and more.

11. Tap Done to close the event. The event will be added to, or updated on, your calendar.

Reading and Responding to a Meeting Invitation

If you use a Microsoft Exchange account on your iPad and you have Calendars enabled for Exchange, you can receive and respond to meeting invitations from people in the same organization using the Calendar app.

An invitation appears on your calendar with a dotted line around it, and the Inbox tray icon in the upper-left corner of your screen shows the number of invitations you have.

Follow these steps to reply to an invitation.

 LET ME TRY IT

Reading and Responding to a Meeting Invitation

1. Find the invitation in the calendar, in the Inbox, or in an email message, and tap it.

2. To send an email to the organizer, tap Invitation From. Tap the email address that appears to send a message to the host.

3. To see who's invited, tap Invitees. Tap a name to see another invitee's contact information, and tap the email address that appears to send a message.

4. To add comments visible to the meeting organizer, tap Add Comments, and type in your comments. Your comments also appear in the info screen for the meeting. Make sure your comments are suitable to be viewed by everyone present!

5. To set an alert for the meeting, tap Alert, and set an alert as you would for a meeting you create.

6. To respond, tap Accept, Maybe, or Decline.

    The response is sent to the meeting organizer, along with any comments you've added. If you choose Accept or Maybe, you can change your response later, and change or add comments by tapping Add Comments.

Following Another Person's Calendar

You can have another person's calendar entries appear on your calendar. This is useful for coordinating schedules with anyone—a boss, a coworker who you've teamed up with on a project, or your significant other or computer-savvy children.

To follow another person's calendar, it needs to be published in either the Mac's iCalendar format (file suffix .ics) or a format called CalDAV. Also, the events from the calendar you're following are read-only. You can read the events, but you can't edit them. You also can't create new events in the other person's calendar, and you can't accept invitations from CalDAV accounts.

You can publish calendars from several services. Google, Yahoo!, and the Mac's iCal program all publish in either format. You can also subscribe to iCalendar calendars published in .ics format on the Web. A link to the calendar arrives in an email link; just click it to subscribe to the calendar.

Follow these steps to subscribe to a published calendar.

 LET ME TRY IT

Subscribing to a Published Calendar

1. From the iPad Home screen, choose Settings.

2. Choose Mail, Contacts, Calendars; then tap Add Account.

3. Choose Other; then, choose either Add CalDAV Account, or for iCalendar, Add Subscribed Calendar. (The screen for Add Subscribed Calendar is shown in Figure 9.10.) For Add CalDAV Account, enter the server name, username and password, and the description. For iCalendar, enter the server name and pathname of the calendar file.

4. Enter the address of the published calendar in the Server box; then tap Next. Your iPad verifies the address and displays the subscription configuration screen.

5. Tap Save. Your iPad creates a new Subscribed Calendar section in the Mail, Contacts, Calendars screen. It adds your subscribed calendar to the new section.

You may want to temporarily remove a subscribed calendar so that it doesn't clutter up your own. Or you may want to delete it.

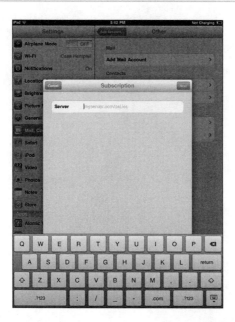

Figure 9.10 *Subscribe to an iCal calendar by entering its server address in the Subscription screen.*

Follow these steps to disable or delete a published calendar.

 LET ME TRY IT

Disabling or Deleting a Published Calendar

1. From the iPad Home screen, choose Settings.

2. Choose Mail, Contacts, Calendars; then tap Subscribed Calendars.

3. Tap the calendar. An Account slider to disable the calendar and the Delete Account button appear.

4. To disable the calendar, slide the Account switch to Off.

5. To delete the calendar, tap Delete Account. When the iPad asks you to confirm, tap Delete Account again.

In this chapter you learn how to interact with web pages directly through touch, scrolling, zooming, saving, and more. You also learn how to save a web page to the Home screen and work with online forms.

10

Surfing the Web on Your iPad

In a recent hit movie, *The Adjustment Bureau*, the "adjusters" of the title use a kind of magic book to track the progress of individuals' fates in the sectors for which they're responsible. The book is alive, changing, and updating as circumstances dictate. That magic book looks an awful lot like an iPad.

Using the Web via touchscreen is somehow more personal and more involving than using it on a personal computer. The large screen of the iPad really brings the Web to life, giving it added breadth and depth. You interact directly with web information and images on your iPad. Using a link by tapping it to bring up the new page feels a bit magical. Panning, zooming, and scrolling are all a lot of fun.

There are also some frustrations with using the Web on the iPad. The iPhone and iPad famously don't support Flash, a multimedia technology from Adobe that's used for posting many web videos online, among other purposes. You probably know what Flash is from having it crash when surfing the Web on your personal computer, rendering many videos—and many ads—unusable.

You never have that problem on the iPad because it doesn't support Flash at all. You either get your video, but delivered via a different technology, which is fine, or you get a message telling you that the video isn't available.

There are other issues. Some web pages are designed for a laptop widescreen and may force you to scroll horizontally to see the whole page. Or the page may just render badly.

All these problems, though, are being fixed as site developers realize what an important part of their audience iPad and other tablet users make up. YouTube quickly changed its video display technology so that HTML5, which is the main alternative to Flash for video display, is used instead of Flash when an iPad is the client machine. More and more sites are following YouTube's lead.

All this just keeps decreasing the hassle factor, and supporting the fun factor, of using the web "live" on a touchscreen. I wouldn't be surprised if the kids of today, many of whom are growing up using iPads, end up considering it odd to use the Web any other way.

Surfing Web Pages

You may well have tried using the Web on a mobile phone—and ended up limiting your mobile web usage in frustration. The small screen of a mobile phone just doesn't handle the full web very well. Some sites are hard to use, or even unusable on mobile phones. Many site owners have created special, limited versions of their sites for use by phones, but that's not much fun either.

Safari is the built-in web browser that comes with the iPad, and it's the one discussed and demonstrated here. However, Safari has some limitations; the main one being that it doesn't support tabs and enables you to only have nine open windows at once. That sounds like a lot, but you may end up filling the nine "slots" with open pages and want more. Alternative browsing apps, available in the App Store, support tabs, ad blocking, and other advanced features. See Chapter 17 "Working with Apps and the App Store," for more about getting apps for your iPad.

The iPad is a different story. The screen resolution, 1024 x 768, is a standard computer screen resolution, so most web pages display well on it. (Some pages are designed for laptop widescreens, which are typically 1280 x 1024 and may be wider than the available space on the iPad screen.) Not only that, but the extra room on the iPad's screen completely changes the experience. Panning and zooming—a grim necessity on small mobile phone screens—is fun on the iPad. The Web feels like it's at your beck and call.

The following sections of this chapter show you specifically how to use your iPad to navigate web pages. Start by tapping the Safari icon on your iPad Home screen. It's one of the apps docked at the bottom of the page by default. Figure 10.1 shows the Safari web browser screen and highlights its key features.

Scrolling a web page is easy—just flick to make the page go in the direction you want. Scrolling up and down is easy and fun; scrolling from side to side is more difficult because it's hard to keep the context in one's mind when the horizontal scrolling is used. It's also hard to read text when each line of the text doesn't entirely fit on the screen horizontally. To reduce or, in some cases, eliminate side to side scrolling, turn the iPad horizontally, and use it in landscape mode. This gives you a wider view of the page—1024 pixels instead of 768, one-third more.

To zoom in and out, place two fingers—or a thumb and one finger—onscreen. Spread them apart to zoom in, or squeeze them together to zoom out. You can often zoom to the width of a column of text or an image by double-tapping the screen. In most cases, the screen resizes so that the current column of text, or the current image, fills the width of the screen in front of you. (In landscape mode, I can sometime read a web page without my glasses after I zoom in on a column of text this way.)

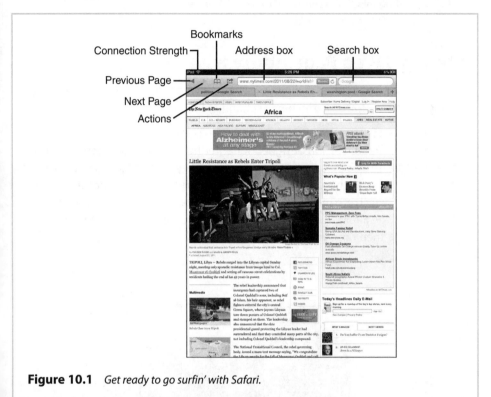

Figure 10.1   *Get ready to go surfin' with Safari.*

To move directly to the top of a web page, tap the status bar in Safari. Tap carefully above icons, such as the Pages or Bookmarks icon, or you activate the icon instead.

 SHOW ME   Media 10.1—A Quick Tour Through Safari
Access this video file through your registered Web Edition at
my.safaribooksonline.com/9780132709590/media
or on the DVD for print books.

TELL ME MORE   Media 10.2—Delving into Your Music Syncing
Options

Access this audio recording through your registered Web Edition at
my.safaribooksonline.com/9780132709590/media
or on the DVD for print books.

Entering a Web Page Address

You can enter web addresses directly into Safari, as described here, or use bookmarks, as demonstrated in the next section.

When you start Safari and tap in the address box, your onscreen keyboard changes
to a slightly different version designed for entering web page addresses, as shown
in Figure 10.2. There's no spacebar, and you see a key labeled .com and a backslash
key. Tap and hold on the .com key, and you see four related keys: .net, .edu, org,
and .us, all of which are more or less commonly used in web page addresses. To
select one of the alternatives, drag your finger from the .com key to the alternative
key you want; then raise your finger.

Figure 10.2   *The Safari browser offers a special keyboard for entering web page addresses.*

To return to a page you previously visited, type part of the page name in the Address box. (No spaces, though, as the keyboard displayed for entering addresses doesn't offer them.) The page appears in a drop-down list beneath the Address box as a choice you can select.

You're likely to enter many web addresses directly into the address box. Safari uses previously entered addresses to prompt you, making entry easier in many cases.

 LET ME TRY IT

Entering a Web Page Address

1. Tap inside the address box. The search box grabs the cursor; you may need to tap inside the address box twice to get the cursor to go there.

2. If there's already a web address in the box, tap the X to clear it. The address box clears.

3. Start typing the web address you want. You can usually skip entering www. at the beginning of the web address. If you type characters that are part of web addresses you've used before, or part of the name of a page that you've used before, Safari displays the web addresses and page names in a list beneath the address box, as shown in Figure 10.3.

4. If the web address you want appears in the list beneath the address box, choose it. If not, type the entire address; then tap Go. Your iPad displays the web page.

One of the few areas where the iPad 2 has substantial advantages over the original iPad may be in web surfing. The iPad 2 has a faster processor, a faster graphics engine, and more memory. All these features speed the display of three popular types of apps: web browsers, maps, and games. The increased memory also reduces the likelihood that Safari will crash during a session. If it does crash, just restart it; it generally returns to where you left off.

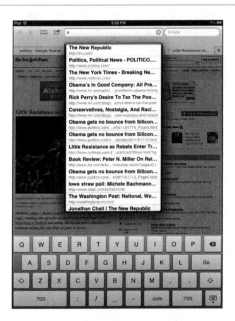

Figure 10.3   *Safari helps by prompting you with related addresses you've used before.*

Using Tabs in Safari

Tabs for the Safari browser on the iPad, as shown in Figure 10.1 and other figures in this chapter, work similarly to tabs on a web browser on a personal computer. Tabs enable you to easily move among different open windows.

One difference between Safari on the iPad and a web browser on a computer, though, is the number of separate browser windows you can have open. Safari on the iPad only allows you to have one open browser window, albeit with as many tabs as you'd like. A web browser on a personal computer allows you to have multiple windows, each with as many tabs as you'd like.

Managing tabs is fairly simple:

- To open a new tab, tap the + button. The new tab opens.

- To close the currently open tab, tap the X in the tab name. The tab closes. (You can re-open it via the History function, described below.)

- To move to a different tab, tap the tab name. The tab opens.

- To move to a previously visited web page within a tab, tap the Back button. To move forward again among your visited tabs, tap the Forward button.

The iPad doesn't impose a hard limit on the number of tabs you use at once. However, every web page that you keep open takes a certain amount of the iPad's memory.

At a certain point—which varies depending on the totality of what's running on your iPad—the iPad's memory will fill up, and the risk of Safari crashing increases. If Safari crashes, you may or may not lose your tab set, and return to a single tab.

There's also a practical limit to the number of tabs you want to open because it becomes more and more difficult to identify tabs (from very short labels) and to select a different tab by tapping it (because the label is so small). The practical limit seems to me to be about 10 tabs.

If you're like me, you might find yourself opening numerous tabs during a session and leaving them open when you get distracted and start doing something else—either on the iPad, or in the rest of your life. You may then feel frustrated, when you return to Safari, to see open tabs whose purpose you've forgotten and, frankly, don't care about.

Consider keeping the number of open tabs to a small number—perhaps four or five—to reduce headaches associated with using and managing tabs, and to reduce the risk of having Safari crash.

Using Web Links and Saving Photos

Clicking links accounts for much of the joy of using the Web. Much of the reason it's called "web surfing" is the free and flexible feeling of moving smoothly from one page to another. It's always good to have options, though, including when you encounter a web link you want to use. Experienced web users are familiar with right-clicking (or on the Mac, command-clicking) to see a range of options for a web link.

The equivalent to right-clicking the iPad is to tap and hold to see options. One of the options is to open the web page at the other end of the link in a new browser window. When you choose this option, Safari closes the current page temporarily, shows you a graphic with all open pages, and then opens the new page. To return to the previous page, tap the Pages icon; then choose the previous page from among the page images.

Following links, using options, and saving images are described in the following steps.

LET ME TRY IT

Using Links in Safari

1. When you see a link, tap and release to follow it without seeing options. The browser window refreshes with the destination page's contents; in some cases, the link automatically opens in a new window, even if you don't choose that option. This can be surprising; if you already have nine windows open in Safari, and the new window opening causes you to lose one of the previously open ones, it can be downright frustrating. Google News at news.google.com is an example of a website that always opens links in a new window.

2. Tap and hold a link to see options.

   Options appear—usually Open, Open in New Page and Copy as shown in Figure 10.4.

   The destination URL displays above the options. If the URL doesn't look like a website that you want to go to, tap Cancel.

Figure 10.4 *Safari gives you options when you tap and hold a link.*

3. To open the link as if you had simply tapped it, tap Open. To open the link in a new page, tap that option. To copy the link address for use in another

program or another browser window, tap Copy. To return to the page you were visiting, tap Cancel.

Safari opens the new web page—in the same window or another window, depending on what you choose—or copies the web address to its internal clipboard.

If you've opened the link in a new page, the Pages icon displays the new number of currently open pages—one more than previously shown.

4. To save an image that appears on a web page, tap and hold on the image. From the options that appear, choose Save Image. The image is saved to the Camera Roll album for your iPad. To view the image, from the Home screen, tap the Photos icon; then tap Camera Roll.

   If the image is a link, the destination web address displays in the list of options, just as it does for other links. In this case, you can also open the destination page, open it in a new window, or copy the destination address—not the photo.

5. If you opened the link in a new page and want to return to the previous page, press the Pages icon—the one with a number on it. The currently open pages display, as shown in Figure 10.5.

6. To finish returning to the previous page, or to go to a different page, select it from among the icons on display. The selected page opens in the browser.

Figure 10.5   *Safari shows you the pages it currently has open.*

Using History and Bookmarks

You can get to previously visited web pages using Safari on your iPad in three ways:

- **Predictive prompts:** While typing in the address bar, Safari produces a list of recently visited pages that match the characters being typed, as described in the previous section. Either the URL or the page title can provide the match. A few characters is usually enough to retrieve the needed site.

- **History:** Safari keeps track of pages you've visited and when and makes that information available to you in a list under the Bookmarks icon, as shown in Figure 10.6. To access the list, just press the Bookmarks icon, tap the History folder (if it's not already open from a previous access), and then tap your way to the page you're looking for. To clear history, tap the Clear History button.

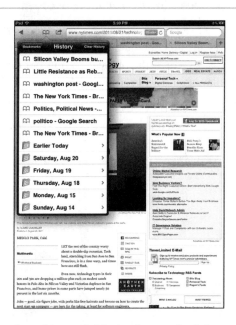

Figure 10.6 *To get to your history of visited web pages, begin by tapping the Bookmarks icon; then tap History if needed.*

 SHOW ME   Media 10.3—A History of Your Web Surfing
Access this video file through your registered Web Edition at
my.safaribooksonline.com/9780132709590/media
or on the DVD for print books.

- **Bookmarks:** Safari enables you to put bookmarks in a list or in a Bookmarks Bar, as shown in Figure 10.6. To access a bookmark, simply tap it. To edit bookmarks, press the Edit button. Then press the red minus symbol to delete a bookmark, or drag the Towers of Hanoi icon—three stacked disks—to re-order the entries.

To clear out the history files for Safari, bring up the history pane, and then tap the Clear History button. The history clears—not only the list of sites you visited and when, but also the predictive prompts for websites that appear when you start to type a web address in the address bar. This is useful for preventing coworkers who admire your iPad, for instance, from seeing that you've been looking at help wanted ads from your company's competitors.

The predictive prompts provided in the address bar and the History function are automatic. The next section describes in detail how to add a bookmark and how to synchronize bookmarks with other platforms.

You can also search the web using the search box. Just tap in the search box and enter the search terms you want to use. Google then looks in its index for pages that most closely match the terms you enter, just like on a personal computer; it even recalls recent entries you've made (see Figure 10.7).

Figure 10.7 *Google search works just as well on the iPad as on a personal computer, opening up the whole Web for you.*

Tap and release on a link in the search results to update the current browser window with the destination page. Tap and hold to see alternative actions, which include opening the web page in the current browser window, opening the web page in a new browser window, and copying the link address for use elsewhere.

Adding Bookmarks

Bookmarks save time and hassle. They replace the somewhat laborious process of entering a web address in Safari with a few quick taps. There are two complementary ways to get bookmarks into Safari on your iPad. One way is to import them from your browser on a Macintosh or Windows PC. The other way is to add bookmarks as you go along. Use both techniques to build up your Bookmarks list.

I may be unusual in this regard, but I seldom use history and bookmarks on my iPads. (I have an original iPad and an iPad 2 as well.) However, I use history and bookmarks on my laptop all the time. I think this reflects the fact that I use the iPad as a kind of portable newspaper or magazine, so I visit the same few sites over and over. My favorite iPad sites are mostly news and politics sites, the weather, and an occasional quick hit of information about someplace I'm going. If I want to do something more with a page, I email the URL to myself for further work on my laptop—or leave the page open in Safari and then search for the same page on my laptop.

The only browser supported for Windows PCs, at this writing, is Internet Explorer. If you use a different browser, you may want to import its bookmarks into Internet Explorer and then synchronize bookmarks with your iPad. See the online help for IE to see how to do this for your browser.

You can also add and remove bookmarks to make the list suitable for use on your iPad. Then sync from the web browser on the personal computer to Safari on the iPad.

You should also be mindful, though, that you may end up using a different browser than Safari on your iPad. Tabbed browsing, in particular, is natural for use on a touchscreen, and Safari doesn't have it; other iPad browsers do.

Some other browsers also support Adobe's Flash technology, such as web pages that use Flash to put video onscreen. You simply can't see such videos when you use Safari on the iPad; with some other browsers, you can.

There are several good competing web browser apps available in the App Store, and you may fall for one of them. In that case, the work you do to get bookmarks into Safari on your iPad may turn out to be at least partly wasted. However, it's nice to have any browser seeded with the links from your personal computer, so you might as well just get it done.

Safari makes it easy to add bookmarks, either to a menu-like list under the Bookmarks button or onto a Bookmarks Bar. The Bookmarks Bar shows only when you first open a browser window, however. You can't use the Bookmarks Bar from a window that you're already using; you have to open a new window instead.

I find the Bookmarks Bar in Safari annoying; it seems to take up badly needed space when a window opens and then isn't available onscreen when I do decide that I want to use it. As a result, I never put anything new in the Bookmarks Bar and never use it. I'm sure that many other iPad users, possibly including yourself, will be avid users of the Bookmarks Bar.

You can also use the Actions icon, shown previously in Figure 10.1, for several other actions:

- To add a Page icon to the Home screen. A Web Page icon is added to the Home screen, with a name you can edit. This is a convenient feature, especially because you can now put these icons, and app icons, in folders on the Home screen to organize them.

- Mail links to this page. An email message opens with the Subject preset to the name of the page and the contents being the link to the page. Your email address (for the user account currently active on your iPad) is provided as a cc: page.

- You can specify the number of copies to print and which printer to use.

Follow these steps to add a bookmark.

 LET ME TRY IT

Adding a Bookmark in Safari—and More

1. When you reach a web page that you want to save as a bookmark, tap the Actions icon. A list of actions appears, as shown in Figure 10.8.

2. To create a bookmark, tap Add Bookmark.

    The Add Bookmark pane appears, as shown in Figure 10.9.

Figure 10.8 *You can do several things with an open web page, including adding a bookmark for it.*

Figure 10.9 *You can rename a bookmark before saving it.*

3. To rename the bookmark, use the keyboard to enter the new name. Now take a look at the bottom of the Add Bookmark pane, as shown in Figure 10.9. If it says Bookmarks, your bookmark will be saved in the Bookmarks list; if it says Bookmarks Bar, your bookmark will be saved there instead.

   The next step tells you how to change where your bookmark will go.

4. If Bookmarks is showing at the bottom of the Add Bookmark page, and you want to put the bookmark into the Bookmarks Bar instead, tap Bookmarks to open the Bookmarks pane; then tap Bookmarks Bar in the pane. If Bookmarks Bar is showing at the bottom of the Add Bookmark page, and you want to put the bookmark into the Bookmarks list instead, tap Bookmarks Bar to open the Bookmarks pane; then tap Bookmarks in the pane. Tap Add Bookmark to return.

   This is potentially confusing; many people may end up putting bookmarks in the place where they didn't want them.

5. Tap Save to add the bookmark.

Synchronizing Bookmarks

You may have an impressive and, more important, useful list of bookmarks on a personal computer. Use these steps to transfer the bookmarks to Safari on your iPad.

Follow these steps to synchronize bookmarks between Safari on a personal computer and Safari on the iPad.

 LET ME TRY IT

Synchronizing Bookmarks in Safari

1. Connect your iPad to your Macintosh or Windows PC.

2. In iTunes, in the sidebar on the left, look for your iPad in the Devices branch. iTunes displays the Summary tab.

3. Click the Info tab. iTunes displays the Info tab, as shown in Figure 10.10.

4. For a Windows PC, click the Sync Bookmarks With check box to activate it, and then choose your Windows PC web browser from the list that appears. (At this writing, the only browser that appears is Internet Explorer.) For a Mac, click the Sync Safari Bookmarks check box.

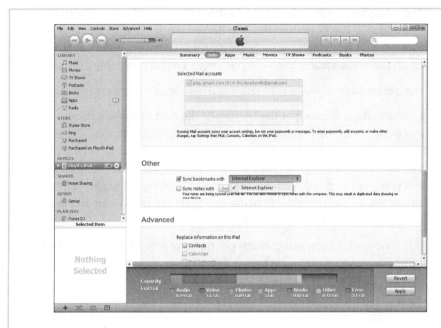

Figure 10.10 *iTunes can sync to many browsers.*

5. Click Apply. iTunes synchronizes bookmarks from your computer to Safari on your iPad.

6. When the sync is complete, click the Eject icon next to the name of your iPad in the iTunes Devices list.

Using the Reading List and Reader

Reading is a very popular use of the iPad, and reading from a web browser is made much easier with the Reading List and the Reader.

The Reading List saves a currently open web page into a list that you can manage, much like your list of bookmarks. You can ease the burden of managing tabs by saving pages you want to read in the Reading List, and then using the tab that the page had been occupying for something else.

The Reader simply extracts the text from a web page and presents it in an easily readable format, in which you can increase or decrease the font size. See Figure 10.11 for an example.

It's a little odd to use the Reader at first, because you see the page's content out of context. However, many web pages are so crowded with navigation and/or ads that they're hard to read, especially on the iPad (because the screen is smaller than most computer screens). Reader can be very useful for breaking free of screen clutter.

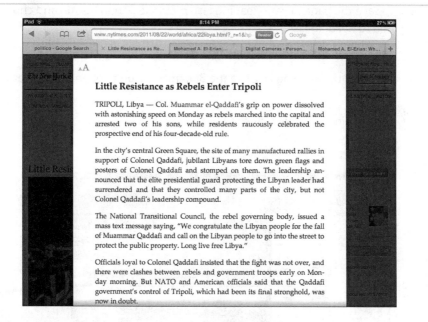

Figure 10.11   *The Reading List adds a whole new dimension to Safari.*

You may find yourself wishing that the Reading List saved a copy of the web page you were viewing, so it worked faster and worked offline. If that's what you want, a third-party app called Instapaper provides it. Instapaper has both free and paid versions. If you're interested, look it up in the App Store (see Chapter 17 for more on the App Store).

 LET ME TRY IT

Using the Reading List and Reader in Safari

1. Open Safari on your iPad.

2. Open a web page.

3. To see the main content of the page in Reader, press the Reader button in Safari's address bar.

   The main content of the page opens.

4. To save the page in your Reading List, press the Action button and choose Add to Reading List.

   The page is added to your reading list.

5. To access the Reading List, tap the Bookmarks icon to open it. Tap Reading List.

   The Reading List opens, as shown in Figure 10.12.

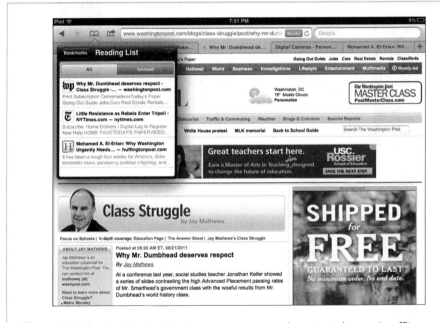

Figure 10.12   *The Reading List gives you access to web content when you're offline.*

6. Tap All to see all Reading List stories. Tap Unread to see unread stories.

7. To open a story, tap its description in the Reading List.

   The web page with the story opens.

In this chapter you learn how to find locations on the map and how to get directions.

11

Making the Most of Maps

The movie *The Adjustment Bureau*, mentioned in the previous chapter, featured a couple trying to keep their romance together, even though it didn't fit into a kind of cosmic plan for humanity. The couple survived various intercessions designed to keep them apart but eventually got the plan changed so they could be together. It was a fun and interesting love story, but what got me hooked was the Sector Book.

This was a book with a kind of interactive map on it that showed the fate of various characters as they moved through the landscape around them. I kept waiting for the book to show up again in the movie and researched it online afterward. (Yes, I know—pretty nerdy.)

The iPad is very much like that magical Sector Book. It contains, or can access, an amazing amount of information. It's fully interactive, especially when it's connected to the Internet.

One of the ways in which this magic plays out most powerfully is with the Maps application. It's very cool to pan and zoom around a lively, interactive map. The Street Maps feature in Google Maps, displayed on a large screen, is almost worth the price of admission by itself.

It's even more amazing, if you have an online connection, to use the map as you move toward your destination. If not, you can get almost the same result, but it takes advance planning and preparation—as described in this chapter.

With the iPad and the Maps app, you can find all sorts of destinations, get information about them, get directions from one place to another, see traffic information mapped onscreen, and more.

Understanding Mapping and Connectivity

The Maps app, in concert with your iPad hardware, does two main things: shows you a location (including your current location) and shows you how to get from one place to another. The kind of iPad you have affects this functionality in a way that's a little confusing.

The best case for navigation is that you have a 3G iPad, which has GPS in the same module as the Wi-Fi hardware. Almost as good is to have a Wi-Fi iPad tethered to a smartphone with built-in GPS; the GPS signal is passed to your iPad. The only problem with this arrangement is that it quickly runs down your phone's battery.

With a 3G iPad, or a Wi-Fi iPad tethered to a smartphone with GPS, you have nearly constant access to both location information and new maps downloaded to your iPad as you need them. This is a marvelous setup and interacts with other iPad goodness, such as your Contacts information, the big touchscreen on your iPad, its long battery life, and so on, to make for a nearly ideal digital map.

The only thing that the iPad mapping capability lacks, when you have a live Internet connection, is full turn-by-turn navigation. This is a sophisticated capability that you need to pay extra for by buying an app that supports it. (The app works better if you have a 3G iPad or an iPad tethered to a smartphone with GPS.) On Android smartphones and tablets, by contrast, turn-by-turn navigation is also included in the navigation capability. The iPad is still superior in many ways to these other devices, and it does do a lot with navigation—it even shows traffic information, as described later. But free turn-by-turn navigation is one feature that Android has to itself.

Things are a bit trickier if you have a Wi-Fi-only iPad and take it out of your home or office, away from familiar Wi-Fi networks. On the go, it's unlikely that you'll have continuous access to Wi-Fi. There will be Wi-Fi networks around in most places, but most of them will be private and password-protected, so you cannot use them.

Your Wi-Fi-only iPad can still get location information in many places—ironically, it gets location information by mapping Wi-Fi base stations against a database of their locations. But without a data connection, you cannot get map data onto your iPad, so it may very well know where you are but cannot plot that information onto a map.

To work around this—or to avoid hassling with the map while in transit—you can do a couple of things:

- **Get detailed directions to your location onto your iPad:** Get the directions and a suitable map to display onscreen, as shown in Figure 11.1. Then, use the onscreen display for your trip, even if it can't be updated by new information. If you have printer access from your iPad, you can print the information as well.

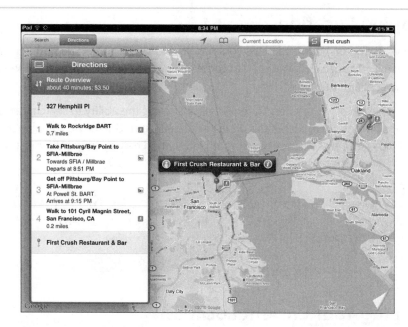

Figure 11.1   *You can "preload" your iPad with a relevant map and directions.*

- **Print directions from a personal computer:** Get directions and a map ready before you go. If you have access to a personal computer, the Google Maps service at maps.google.com not only makes it easy to get the needed information, but it also prints out directions (but not maps) in a way that fits nicely onto a printout.

Street View is a marvelous capability of Google Maps and it looks and works better on the iPad than on any other available computer, phone, or other device. Having a photographic environment you can move around in is cool enough, in the many locations for which Street View is available. But having that on a big, high-resolution screen that you can easily carry with you and use by a touch-screen is a lot of fun and very useful. Better still, it's integrated with your contacts, calendar, and more. Use Street View before you set out to know how to navigate when you're near your destination. And use it after you arrive for an interactive map that actually looks like what you see around you.

I recommend that you not put yourself in the position of urgently needing a data connection when you get near your destination—and quite possibly not being able to find one. A few minutes of prep work can save you a lot of stress in getting where you're going safely.

Mapping Locations

The Maps app on your iPad helps you map your current location and other locations that you specify. Locations can come from your Contacts app as well, which can be convenient.

The Maps app also provides related services, such as the ability to search near a location, for instance, to find the pizza parlor nearest to the movie you plan to see. The iPad's large screen and easy, smooth interaction helps you get the most out of its mapping capabilities.

The original iPad is great for mapping, but the iPad 2 is even better. The newer device is thinner and lighter and is smaller than many printed map books you might buy. It's also faster and has more memory, so you're more likely to get the map you need onscreen as soon as you need it.

Mapping Your Current Location

You often want to find your current location. The classic case of this is when you don't know where you are. But you also want to find your current location when you're in a familiar location, such as home, as a starting point for searching nearby or getting directions.

The Maps app makes this much easier than using a paper map or a map book. With a paper map, you have to look for nearby street names or landmarks, find those in the map, and gradually narrow down the possibilities to find your specific location. It's much easier with the Maps app.

When you start the Maps app, it may first ask you whether it can use your current location; be sure to press OK. (This is a privacy protection step.) Maps then shows your current location as a blue dot and displays a map of the area around you, as shown in Figure 11.2. Wham! You've located yourself.

If you're on the move when you do this, you see the blue dot moving on the map. One of the problems with navigating with your iPad while walking is that you don't move fast enough to quickly jog the blue dot along, so it's harder to infer your direction. Zoom in tightly and then walk a few steps to help solve this problem.

One thing you'll find yourself doing as you use Maps out in the real world is panning and zooming the map to see the area around you. You can move the focus of the map such that it no longer shows your location. To recenter the map around where you are now, press the Tracking icon, which looks like a blue arrowhead (and which is pointed out in Figure 11.2). The map refreshes and recenters around you.

Tracking icon

Figure 11.2   *The blue dot in Maps shows you where you are.*

Double-tap the Tracking icon to turn compass mode on and off. Compass mode forces the map to stay oriented such that north is at the top of your iPad; the Tracking icon shows as a blue arrow. With compass mode off, the map tries to orient itself to the direction you're pointing or heading, and the Tracking icon updates to show a blue fan in front of the arrow. (As you can tell, I like compass mode and always leave it on.)

Mapping a Place or an Address

Besides your current location, which is always just a tap away (via the Tracking icon), you can always enter another location in several ways:

- **Entering an address:** You can enter an address directly. This might be asking a lot of the Maps app—there are a lot of "Main Streets" in the world—but you can help by including the city or town and, if needed, the state and/or country. (The Maps app can decode such abbreviations as "sf", "nyc," and "la.")

- **Entering a place name:** You can also enter a place name, followed by a city and possibly a state and/or country name as well. The Maps app does surprisingly well with finding a lot of places by name, but you may end up having to enter the address instead.

- **Entering a contact name:** You can begin to enter a contact name, and the Maps app quickly homes in on the contact you want. Remember to try this when you're using Maps; it's fun and easy.

- **Entering a type of place:** You can search for "coffee," "chocolate," or other types of places, and Maps brings up suggestions, shown as pushpins. Tap a pushpin for more information.

- **Direct navigation:** This is an often-ignored but convenient option. You can pan and zoom the map to move to the location you want and then drop a pin on the location to mark it. (Dropping a pin is described later.)

The steps for entering an address, place name, or contact name are given here. For entering a type of place, see the "Using Search Nearby" section. For direct navigation, just try it!

 LET ME TRY IT

Mapping a Place or an Address

1. In the Maps app, tap inside the box, Search or Address. Maps displays the Search screen.

2. Type the name of the location, the name of a contact, or the address. Maps prompts you with suggestions based on your previous entries as you type; select from the scrolling list if your desired entry appears.

3. If Maps doesn't understand your entry right away, it may show you a list of options and ask you to choose—if so, choose the right option, or tap Cancel and re-enter the address. Figure 11.3 shows an example of options.

4. Tap Search. The Maps app finds the location and adds a red pushpin to the map to show the location, as shown in Figure 11.4. Maps also displays a banner with the location name and two icons—the one on the left for Street View and one on the right for more information.

Figure 11.3 *Maps can helpfully provide options for you to choose from.*

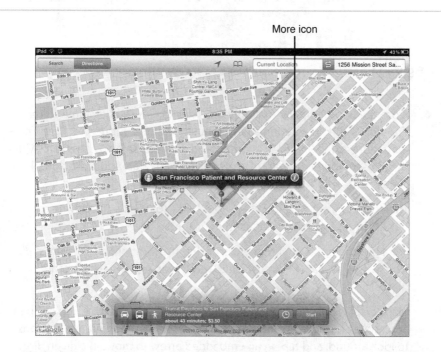

Figure 11.4 *Maps shows you the location and offers much more.*

5. For more information, tap the blue More icon, which has an i character on it (refer to Figure 11.4). The More icon leads to more information, as shown in Figure 11.5. This may include the location's phone number, address, and website. Google Places service provides the data; for more information, see my book, *Teach Yourself Google Places in 10 Minutes* (Sams, 2011).

Figure 11.5   *The Maps app offers quite a bit of information about many places.*

6. From the Location pane that appears (refer to Figure 11.5), tap Add to Contacts to begin entering a new contact, with the address set to the current address. Tap Share Location to send an electronic business card with the chosen address as part of an email message. Tap Add to Bookmarks to create a bookmark of the location.

   These options are easy to miss in your hurry to use the underlying map, but they make the Maps app far more useful.

7. For a photographic environment showing the location, tap the Street View icon, where available (in most cities and towns, and also many other places).

   Maps displays the location in a photographic panorama that you can pan and move around in, as shown in Figure 11.6. Flick in different directions to look around, and tap on an embedded arrow to move in a given direction within Street View.

Figure 11.6   *Street View gives you an amazingly detailed view of many locations.*

8. To drop a pin on an area—that is, to mark it, allowing you to get directions
    for it and more—tap the lower-right corner of the map to see view options,
    as described in the next section. Tap the Drop Pin button.

 SHOW ME   **Media 11.1—Dropping a Pin**
Access this video file through your registered Web Edition at
my.safaribooksonline.com/9780132709590/media
or on the DVD for print books.

Switching to a Different Map View

You'll spend most of your time using the Maps app in the Classic view, which is the
default. However, three other map views are also available.

To access the view options, simply touch the lower-right corner of the screen,
where it looks like the map is rolled up a bit. The map rolls up further and exposes
several different view-related options, as shown in Figure 11.7.

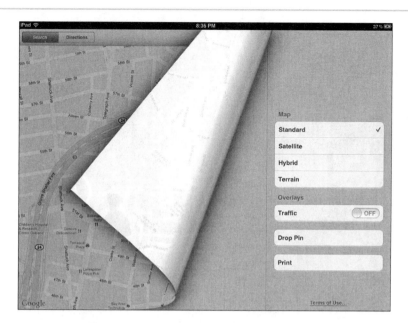

Figure 11.7   *Map options are a bit hidden (tap the lower-right corner of your map) but powerful.*

The additional options follow:

- **Satellite view:** Satellite view is fantastic. It shows how the area you look at appears from a satellite view on a sunny, cloudless day.

- **Hybrid:** Hybrid view, shown in Figure 11.8, adds classic map information, such a street names and business names, to the satellite view. Try this near where you live; you may never look at your neighborhood in quite the same way again.

- **Terrain:** Terrain view combines classic map information and a topographic map showing elevations. This is great for planning bicycle rides and hikes, but it can also show you areas where even a car is likely to move more slowly.

- **Traffic overlay:** You simply slide a little slider over, and traffic information is added to any map you look at. A traffic overlay on the Terrain map is shown in Figure 11.9. People often pay a monthly subscription fee for this kind of information, but you get it for free on the Maps app.

- **Drop Pin:** Dropping a pin puts a pin—a kind of pointer—on a specific spot on the map. After you have a pin, you can get directions and travel times, see Street View for a location (if available), add the address to contacts, share the address, and add it to bookmarks.

Figure 11.8   *The Hybrid view combines satellite imagery and classic cartography.*

- **Print:** You get the ability to send the current map view to a printer. Printer access directly from an iPad is still on the rare side, but if you have printer access, you can use it productively with the Print option.

There are caveats to all these maps. Roads change, business names change even faster, and traffic conditions change fastest of all. Traffic information is always at least somewhat out of date—and no map can answer the questions you want answers to, such as: "How long with it take me to get there?" and "What's the best route to take right now?"

However, big splotches of red across the freeway are a good warning to give yourself more time, consider an alternative route, and start listening to local radio traffic reports for more information. This kind of tip-off can be invaluable.

Getting Directions

Getting directions is the main use people make of the Maps app—and the most challenging, especially if you don't have a Wi-Fi+3G iPad or easy-to-use tethering to a mobile phone available. People tend to be in a hurry when getting directions and are often nervous, because the stakes are so high—getting lost and being late are both potentially quite embarrassing and frustrating.

Having mentioned the difficulties, the Maps app is also a wonderful tool for getting directions. Having a big, interactive touchscreen to work with as you map out your destination and getting different kinds of directions is marvelous.

The only thing lacking from the Maps app is turn-by-turn directions. This is confusing because the Maps app does give you directions that tell you every turn to take.

SHOW ME Media 11.2—Getting Directions
Access this video file through your registered Web Edition at
my.safaribooksonline.com/9780132709590/media
or on the DVD for print books.

What the Maps app doesn't do is read directions to you out loud as you're on the move; it won't tell you, "In 300 feet, turn left" and so on as you travel. This level of nannying isn't necessary on most trips, but it is something that would be awfully nice to have on occasion. If you need this capability, you can easily buy an app that provides it to you. Such apps work best if you have a Wi-Fi+3G iPad or if you're tethered to a mobile phone or MiFi for GPS information.

See Chapter 17, "Working with Apps and the App Store," for more information about purchasing useful apps and the App Store.

The Maps app supports three kinds of directions:

- **Driving:** Driving directions take into account one-way streets, toll routes, and other information that's important to drivers. Use the Traffic overlay to help you plan your trip. (Current traffic information is not integrated into the directions.)

- **Transit:** Impressively, the Maps app supports public transport directions for all sorts of trips. Trips include walking time to bus and train stops and on-transit times. For buses, traffic information can help you anticipate possible delays. Schedules are included, which is convenient, but I suggest that you always check these with other information sources, such as a transit organization's website, before you go.

- **Walking:** Walking directions ignore one-way streets and other car-only concerns and get you straight to where you want to go. Consider using walking directions for driving and transit trips, too, to get you from the parking lot or transit stop to and from your actual destination.

The Maps app will often show you more than one route to a destination. To get directions using an additional route, just tap the name of the route, such as Route 2, on the map.

If you have a Wi-Fi+3G iPad or have tethering available, you can often work on your directions en route. (Not while you are driving, of course!) However, to avoid anxiety and frustration, or if you have a Wi-Fi-only iPad and no tethering, map out your route before you go. Look at the current state of traffic, consider elevation changes (using the Terrain view) if you're on a bicycle or on foot, and find the best, fastest, easiest route. Put the route onscreen, with directions, so you can refer to it as if it were a printed map, but one custom-made just for this trip.

TELL ME MORE   Media 11.3—Understanding What to Expect from Traffic

Access this audio recording through your registered Web Edition at
my.safaribooksonline.com/9780132709590/media
or on the DVD for print books.

There are several ways to get the job done—and you can get directions using different methods to find the starting and ending locations. You can also begin from where you are, from some other location you start from, or from where you want to end up.

These steps show one simple, flexible method to get directions.

LET ME TRY IT

Getting Directions to a Location

1. Using the Search option, find your starting location on the map. If necessary, drop a pin to mark it. Consider adding the location to Bookmarks or Contacts for easier use in the future.

2. Still using Search, find your ending location on the map. Again, if needed, drop a pin to mark it, and consider adding the location to Bookmarks or Contacts for easier use in the future.

3. Tap the Directions button. A screen with Start and End locations appears.

4. Tap in the Start area. A drop-down list of suggested starting points appears, labeled Recents, as shown in Figure 11.9. The list includes your current location and any destinations you recently searched for or dropped a pin on.

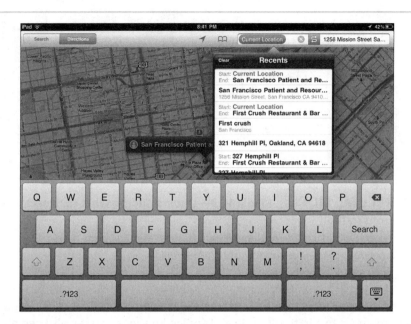

Figure 11.9 *The Recents list for starting and ending points includes dropped pins.*

5. Choose your Start location or type an address, business name, or contact name. Alternatively, press the Bookmarks icon for bookmarks, recents (recently used locations), and contacts. Select the appropriate destination. The starting location appears on the map.

6. Tap in the End area and choose your destination in the same way that you chose your starting point in step 5. The route is shown on the map, centered on the destination.

7. Push the appropriate button to choose from among Auto, Transit, and Walking directions. The directions update to reflect your choice.

8. If needed, tap in the lower-right corner of the map to expose mapping options. Choose mapping options, as described in the previous section. Options include Classic, Satellite, Hybrid, and Terrain maps, and a Traffic overlay for any map you choose.

9. For transit only, push the Time icon to see transit times, as shown in Figure 11.10. Treat the times as a guideline, and double-check them with external sources such as a transit organization's website.

Figure 11.10 *Transit times are just one of the many options you have for directions in Maps.*

10. For step-by-step directions, press the Start button. Then use the arrow buttons to move forward and backward through the directions, one step at a time. The map updates to show each step of your trip.

11. For a list of directions, press the List icon. A list of directions appears, as shown in Figure 11.1 at the beginning of this chapter.

In this chapter you learn how to bring music onto your iPad through iTunes, how to download it directly, and how to play it.

12

Managing Music on Your iPad

The iPad can do so much, but one of its best capabilities tends to get overlooked. Apple's big move into true consumer electronics began with the iPod, more than 10 years ago. The iPhone and the iPad are direct descendants; the famous, multibillion App Store that serves the newer devices so well is just a tab within the iTunes Store, originally devoted entirely to audio.

The music app on the iPad is simply called Music. (It was called iPod, out of respect for the original device, until late 2011, when Apple renamed it.) The Music app makes your iPad into the best iPod ever—a gorgeous, large-screen, full-color iPod with excellent storage capability. (Although music space can quickly get squeezed by other uses, such as movies.)

The iPad also supports multitasking for music. Even the initial software release supported the Music app in the background. Now, any music app can run in the background, keeping the tunes playing while you use other apps. This can be a lot of fun! So music is an additional capability to everything else on the iPad, not an either-or proposition.

The only barrier to using the Music app well is that it takes a bit of work to acquire and manage music so that you have it available when you need it. It's easy to neglect this prep work in your excitement about all the other things the iPad can do. Take the time to do that bit of work before you need it; for your troubles, you can have a powerful addition to everything the iPad can do for you.

There isn't a great way to use your iPad to listen to local radio stations. Many radio station websites offer a "listen live" or similar option, so you could visit a site through Safari, but this capability often doesn't work on the iPad. (This may change over time.) And high-value content like sports games is often not available for free over the Internet, even though it's free (ads notwithstanding) on an actual radio.

The Music app is only one way to play music on your iPad. In earlier versions of the iPad's operating software, though, this app was the only one that would continue playing music in the background when you switched to another task. Other music apps besides iPod would cut out as soon as you switched what was onscreen, which was enough to make them sort of useless in many cases.

Now, however, all apps have access to a background service that can continue playing music or other sounds while you work on other tasks. There are dozens of other apps that bring music in—streamed music over the Internet, stored music, and much more. Most users of these other apps have experience with an actual iPod and the Music app on the iPhone or iPad. After you learn your way around the Music app, you can better deal with these other apps as well.

Synchronizing Music

Millions of people have song libraries built up over many years using iTunes on their Windows PCs and Macs, shared among iPods, iPhones, and now iPads. It's a marvelous ecosystem, allowing you to curate a collection of music, podcasts, video, and audiobooks that means something to you.

Even if you've just started using iTunes to manage your music library, in doing so, you're making an investment in your future with music.

Synchronizing your existing song library to your iPad allows you to leverage your investment in iTunes music over yet another device. The iPad is now the best and the brightest device for iTunes music—it does more than the other devices, it has a much bigger screen, it's fast, and it has great storage capacity.

You can, of course, also use iTunes to find and bring in new music, movies, and more, whether you're adding to an existing collection or starting a new one. The iPad is often criticized for its dependence on a personal computer to do some things, but it makes sense to use your computer—with its faster processing speed, greater storage, and bigger screen—for acquiring and managing music.

The iPad does bend the paradigm, though, if not break it. It's so close to a personal computer in capability that it's easy to use it for acquiring and playing music.

There's a problem with downloading music directly to an "i" device, such as the iPad, though. If you get music on one device, it's not available to the others—including future devices that Apple hasn't even created yet. I recommend that you get as much of your music as possible through iTunes on your personal computer; keep building up that iTunes library for the future.

When you sync your iPad to iTunes, you have two options:

- **Sync everything:** This is quick and easy. The problem is, you may or may not have room on your iPad for your entire iTunes music collection. My advice: Make room! It's a comfort to have your entire collection available on the iPad and, potentially, on other devices as well.

How can you tell if your music collection will fit on your iPad? In iTunes, click the Music category in the iTunes sidebar; then read the size value in the Status bar. Then connect your iPad, look at the iPad in the iTunes Devices list, and read the amount of free space you have. If you don't have room, consider deleting large files, such as TV shows and movies, from your iPad to make room for your music. (Video takes about 10 times the storage per minute as music—10MB/minute versus 1MB/minute. Videos are usually much longer than songs, too.)

- **Sync some:** This takes more gray matter to figure out what to do. You choose playlists, artists, and genres. If you do this, you need to arrange your collection into playlists first before you sync. Doing so can make syncing easier.

If you want to delve deeper into getting iTunes to do more for you, there's an in-depth book with all the gory details. Check out *Using iTunes 10* by Nancy Conner from Que, ISBN 978-0-7897-4787-7.

 TELL ME MORE   Media 12.1—Delving into Your Music Syncing Options

Access this audio recording through your registered Web Edition at
my.safaribooksonline.com/9780132709590/media
or on the DVD for print books.

Get good at keeping your music in sync between your iPad and your personal computer. It can pay off in keeping things simple on all your devices, now and for years to come.

Follow these steps to synchronize music from iTunes to your iPad.

 LET ME TRY IT

Synchronizing Music

1. Connect your iPad to your Windows PC or Macintosh. iTunes opens.

2. In the iTunes sidebar, click your iPad in the Devices list. iTunes displays the Summary tab.

3. Click the Music tab. The Music tab is shown in Figure 12.1.

Figure 12.1 *iTunes lets you sync all your tunes or just selected groups of tunes.*

4. Click the Sync Music check box to activate it.

5. To sync your entire music collection to your iPad, click to choose the Entire Music Library option, and skip to step 8.

6. To sync part of your music collection to your iPad, click to choose the Selected playlists, artists, and genres option.

   Now choose playlists, artists, and genres. To manage this process, create playlists that separate the wheat (what goes on your iPad) from the chaff (everything else).

7. In the Playlists, Artists, and Genres lists, click to make your choices of what content to sync to your iPad.

8. Click Apply. Your choices are used to synchronize the music stored in iTunes on your personal computer to your iPad. Wait while the sync completes.

9. Click the Eject icon next to your iPad's name in the Devices list in iTunes. The syncing completes.

Playing Music with the Music App

The actual iPod device is a marvel, and the Music app on the iPhone is cool, but in many ways, the iPad is better. This is because of the iPad's large touchscreen. The touchscreen makes it easier both to see lots of information and to enter information and commands. It's just a larger control panel to your music and media collection, but that makes a big difference—no pun intended.

One of the coolest things about using the iPad for your music, though, is that, because of iTunes, you have a standard approach to getting, synchronizing, and playing music on your personal computer, iPad and, if you have them (or buy them), your iPod Touch and iPhone. The songs that you can play across all these devices are often referred to as Your iTunes Collection because iTunes is the common denominator.

Although there are lots of other things you can do with your iPad, take the time to learn to use the iPod app. Bringing in music and organizing it does take an up-front investment of time and, if you buy new songs as you go along, money. However, after the work is done, you have a kind of magic radio that's available to you on multiple devices that contains only music that's meaningful to you. The result is special and rewarding.

Navigating the iPod App

To start the iPod app, tap the iPod icon, which appears in the dock of your Home screen. Your library appears—everyone's looks a little different. However, five buttons are always at the bottom of the screen to show five ways to get to your music:

- **Songs:** An alphabetical list of songs. This is good for going to a specific song, and for scanning for interesting songs. If you have more than a few hundred songs, though—and many iPod, iPhone, and iPad users have thousands of songs—scanning gets wearying after a little while.

- **Artists:** Music is arranged by artist. There are likely to be many fewer artists than songs in your music library, so this is a much easier way to scan through a larger collection. See Figure 12.2 for a (brief) example.

- **Albums:** As with the Artists button, Albums drastically cut the number of items you have to look at to navigate your music collection. This is also a good way to get to some of the hidden gems in your collection that may not be the biggest hit songs but are still worthwhile.

- **Genres:** There are potentially dozens of genres, and distinctions can be quite fine. For instance, electronic music, which to me is all one category, includes Industrial, Drum and Bass, and others. Hispanic music includes Alternativo Latino, Regional Mexican, Reggaeton, and Pop Latino. However, only the genres that you have songs in appear, so your genres list is likely to be another effective way into even a large song collection.

- **Composers:** For classical music, this is a strong way into your collection; for popular music, it can be a bit confusing because pop songs are known more by who performed them than who composed them. (Even Bob Dylan, for instance, who has a distinctive songwriting style, did a lot of covers; his songs show up in many other performers' work as well.)

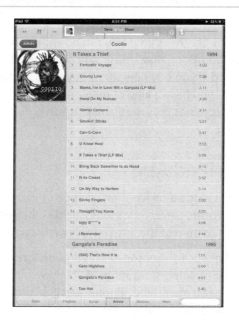

Figure 12.2   *Viewing your tunes by artist makes them easier to find.*

These five categories become more and more important as you pour more and more songs into your iTunes music collection. You may find yourself depending on them quite a bit—and as you think of your music in these categories, you may view your music collection in a new way. The Composer grouping, for instance, is a distinctive way to think about pop songs, rap, and other genres besides classical.

Playing Music

As you build up your song catalog in iTunes, you have the opportunity to play songs back from your personal computer, your iPad, and, if you so choose, an iPod Touch or iPhone. If you have a non-iPhone smartphone, and you don't want to carry your iPad around all the time, you might find it easier to buy an iPod Touch for music playback than to try to integrate your song collection and the way it's organized onto your Android, Blackberry, or other smartphone.

Somewhat to my surprise, a 2011 survey of iPad owners showed that they weren't predominantly iPhone users as well. I had just figured that early iPad sales were mostly from every iPhone user buying one or two iPads. But actually, iPad users are spread fairly evenly across users of all kinds of smartphones and personal computers. Apparently I'm not the only one with a Windows laptop, an Android phone, and at least one iPad. If you have a grab-bag of different kinds of devices, you're far from alone. If your stuff is all Apple, though, and especially if you've been building up your iTunes song catalog for years, life with the iPad is probably a bit easier and more rewarding than otherwise.

There are four ways to listen to songs from your iPad and other devices that support iTunes. You may also listen to music and other audio content through apps such as Pandora, radio station websites, and other means.

For instance, I bought the MLB At Bat app so I can listen to baseball game radio coverage—I actually have Internet access more often than I have reliable radio reception, and I like the infographics in the At Bat app, even if I don't always take the time to look at them. So having an iPad has changed the single biggest reason that I listen to the radio.

Think through how you want to use your music and other audio content, both at home and on the go. Following are the four kinds of output to consider:

- **iPad speaker:** The iPad speaker is surprisingly good, considering its size, but it's not much fun to listen to for a long time. Treat the iPad's speaker as a kind of emergency backup.

- **Regular headset:** I like using a regular headset, and I think it looks a bit less dorky than a Bluetooth headset—which to me makes one look like an alien. However, in-ear speakers hurt after a while, and earmuff-style headsets are bulky and tend to be expensive, requiring careful looking after on the move.

- **Bluetooth headset:** Just like wired headsets, but without the wires, and more expensive. Using a one-ear speakerphone headset is OK for brief periods but becomes limiting after a while.

- **Physical speakers:** Apple offers a variety of ways to hook up regular speakers to an iPad or an iPad stand, and I recommend that you have this option set up for home use. It enables music or other audio to fill your environment without imposing on you as much as music through headphones does.

 LET ME TRY IT

Playing Music

1. In the Music app, tap a category. If the category has subcategories, tap a subcategory.

    For instance, if you choose an artist, composer, or genre, you may then be offered a choice of albums.

2. Tap the song you want to hear.

    The Music app begins playing the song and displays any album art, as shown in Figure 12.3. Note how the album art display takes advantage of the iPad's large screen.

    However, you're free to switch to another app; your music continues playing unless the other app you use takes over background music. If the other app simply has sound effects, as with some games, you hear those along with the music—which can be pleasant or confusing, depending on the specific music, the sound effects, and your mood.

3. To turn the volume up or down, drag the slider in the upper left, or use the iPad's volume rocker switch on the upper-right edge of your iPad (when held upright in portrait mode). If your headphones have a volume control, you can use that as well.

    Using the iPad's volume rocker switch changes the onscreen volume slider. The same thing should occur when you use a volume switch on headphones.

4. To fast-forward or fast-rewind within a song, tap and hold the Rewind or Fast-forward control in the upper right. To move to the beginning or end of the song, tap and release the Rewind or Fast-Forward control.

5. To halt playback, press Pause or the appropriate button on your headset; the control changes to a triangle to indicate Play. To resume playing, press Play or the appropriate button on your headset.

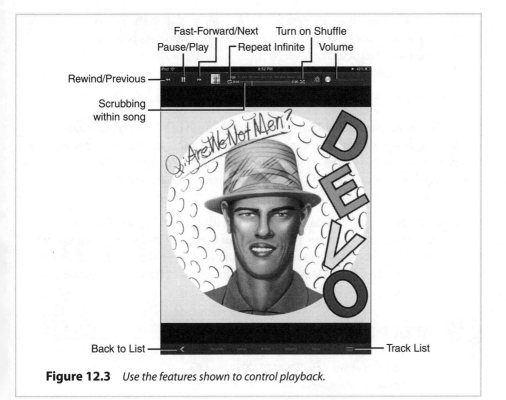

Figure 12.3   *Use the features shown to control playback.*

6. To repeat a song indefinitely, press the Repeat control once. To repeat the song just once, press the Repeat control again.

I really like this one, but friends and family complain when I play the Gorillaz "Feel Good" continually for half an hour. Thank goodness for headphones....

7. To move within a song (called scrubbing), drag the scrubbing control.

If you drag your finger down the screen, you get finer and finer control of the point you move to within the song. This is great for transcribing lyrics or voice recordings.

8. To turn on shuffle mode, tap the Shuffle button—or give your Pad a good shake.

The Shuffle Mode button turns blue. Songs from within the currently chosen list play in random order.

9. To return to the list of tunes, press the Back button.

The current song continues playing until you make another selection.

10. To see the list of tunes instead of the cover art within the playback interface, press the Track List button. The current song continues playing until you make another selection.

Creating a Playlist

You can create playlists in iTunes on your Macintosh or Windows PC, which is where you are more likely to have your complete music collection. It may also be more convenient to work with playlists on a personal computer, where you can use the larger screen, overlapping windows, physical keyboard and mouse, or trackpad to move through a large number of songs more conveniently.

However, you can also create a playlist or Genius Playlist on your iPad. You may want to do this when you are away from your computer and want a quick playlist for an event—or you may choose to make many or all your playlists directly on your iPad. You can use the Music app to create a playlist from the music on your iPad.

 SHOW ME   Media 12.2—Creating a Playlist
Access this video file through your registered Web Edition at
my.safaribooksonline.com/9780132709590/media
or on the DVD for print books.

 LET ME TRY IT

Creating a Playlist

1. In the Music Playlists tab, tap the New icon to create a playlist. The New Playlist pane pops up, requesting a name for the playlist, as shown in Figure 12.4.

2. Use the onscreen keyboard to enter a name for the playlist and tap Save. When you tap Save, a list of your songs appears.

Being painstakingly descriptive may seem boring, but it's likely to help you later when you look at a long list of playlists. Including the date may be a good clue to the list's contents as well.

Figure 12.4 *Use this pane to name your playlists.*

3. Navigate your songs, using the various categories. Clicking the Sources button makes the pop-up shown in Figure 12.5 appear. You can also use the categories buttons long the bottom—Playlists, Songs, Artists, Albums, Genres, and Composers—to quickly scan through your music sorted in different ways.

4. When you see a song you want to add, tap the + button.

5. When you are done, press Done. The playlist appears, as in Figure 12.6.

6. Edit your playlist: Press the minus sign (–) icon to remove a song; drag the song up or down in the list using the Towers of Hanoi icon on the right; tap Add Songs to return to step 3 and add songs. When you finish, press Done.

7. The playlist is saved. To modify it some more, tap Edit.

Creating a Genius playlist is similar to creating a regular playlist, but simpler. Tap the Genius icon instead of the Playlist icon, and just choose one song. Your iPod app creates a playlist of related songs. If you add more songs to your iPad later, tap the Genius playlist, and then tap Refresh; the playlist updates.

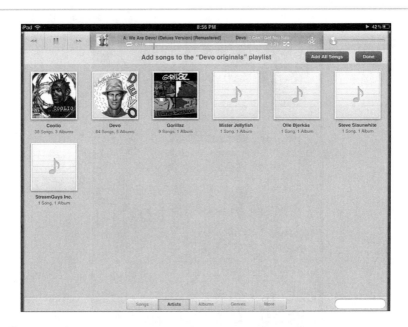

Figure 12.5   *Click the Sources button to choose which collection you are viewing.*

Figure 12.6   *You can edit your playlist, add to it, and complete it.*

13

Making and Receiving FaceTime Calls

FaceTime is a technology that shows off Apple's capabilities at its best. It's the best tool available today for video calls between consumers. It's free to sign up for it and free to use, yet it works better than most videoconferencing systems.

FaceTime is particularly great on the iPad 2. It's not just the built-in cameras that make it work. The faster processor and larger amount of system memory compared to the original iPad make it easier to deliver smooth video and audio performance.

Along with these iPad 2-specific features, the easy transportability of the iPad 2 makes it easier to take advantage of FaceTime, whether around the house or on the go.

FaceTime works only on the iPad 2, not the original iPad. If you have the original iPad, you may want to read this chapter out of interest or because you have access to FaceTime on an iPhone 4 or a Macintosh, but you may also want to skip this chapter.

What's Great About FaceTime

Now take a look at some of the advantages of FaceTime:

- **Free sign-up, free use:** As mentioned, there are no fees for FaceTime—not at sign-up, and not after. It takes advantage of existing infrastructure to operate as a free service.

- **No add-on equipment hassles:** The three supported platforms—newer Macintosh desktop and laptop computers, the iPhone 4, and the iPad 2—all have video cameras (and, of course, display monitors) built in.

- **Easy to use:** As described in this chapter, FaceTime is simple to use. This is a huge plus; people aren't used to video calls as a norm just yet, so making them easy is crucial to adoption.

- **Excellent image quality:** FaceTime delivers excellent image quality and high frame rates, within the limitation that both parties have to be on a wired network (for computers) or using Wi-Fi (for any of the supported platforms).

- **Excellent audio quality:** FaceTime delivers excellent audio quality as well. If you make FaceTime calls in a noisy environment, you might need a headset, but generally you don't.

- **Wi-Fi and 3G support:** When FaceTime first launched, it only worked if both participants were on Wi-Fi networks. Since fall 2011, FaceTime also supports 3G interaction. This is a big plus for users of the iPad 2 and, even more so, for those iPhones that support FaceTime, as iPhones are largely used on the go.

- **Airplay support:** If you have Airplay, which is described in Chapter 1, you can see the contents of your iPad screen on a video display. FaceTime supports Airplay, so you can see the person you're talking to on a big screen.

FaceTime also has imitations. The main one is that it works only on platforms owned by a small percentage of people—newer Macs, the iPhone 4, and the iPad 2. Both parties need one of the right devices handy. Figure 13.1 shows FaceTime running on a big-screen Macintosh.

Figure 13.1 *FaceTime looks great on a big-screen Mac.*

Where possible, I recommend that you consider using a mobile phone as a Wi-Fi hotspot, so you can have a portable Wi-Fi connection for your iPad. (The iPhone 4 supports personal hotspot capability, as do Android mobile phones.) Using a personal hotspot helps Wi-Fi-only iPad users have a mobile connection where they otherwise wouldn't; it even helps Wi-Fi+3G iPad owners by giving them a connection that can do more than using the 3G capability in their iPads. FaceTime is an example of the benefits of this strategy. If you have your iPad connected online directly via 3G, you can't use FaceTime. But if you have a Wi-Fi connection via a mobile phone hotspot, you can. And because Wi-Fi-only iPad owners can also do this, the universe of people who can connect via FaceTime is expanded as well.

You can also connect only with a FaceTime user in the same country you're in. If you are in a different country, you can tell FaceTime what country you're in, and it enables you to make FaceTime calls within that country.

Given these limitations, you can't routinely get into the habit of using FaceTime. You have to plan FaceTime calls with people you know who have the requisite equipment and are interested in having their image beamed across the Internet during a phone call.

It may be that only approximately 10% of people in the United States have the right hardware and network connection at any given time. Because both people need to meet the conditions, only approximately 1% of all U.S. phone calls have the option to be conducted via FaceTime.

But this is how Apple usually starts things out. The original iPod worked only with Macintosh computers when it launched—and among them, only young people showed much interest. Apple worked hard to get the user experience right, and then gradually expanded its universe until the iPod became the huge hit that helped give rise to the iPhone and, now, the iPad.

If FaceTime catches on within its current target audience, don't be surprised if Apple makes it available for other platforms over time. Eventually, millions of people might use FaceTime for a good share of what used to be phone calls. And because the iPad is the best FaceTime device, and likely to remain so, FaceTime would help sell a lot of iPads that way.

As an early adopter, given that you have an iPad 2 and, perhaps some interest, try to use FaceTime as often as you can. Why? A video phone call makes a phone call that much more like an in-person meeting.

By using FaceTime now, you not only get the benefit of video, but you also gain experience with video phone calls for the day that they become more popular. As an early adopter of FaceTime, you can gain experience that may help you, and those around you, as video phone calls become more widely available.

 TELL ME MORE   **Media 13.1—Understanding the Advantages of FaceTime Calls**

Access this audio recording through your registered Web Edition at
my.safaribooksonline.com/9780132709590/media
or on the DVD for print books.

Creating Your FaceTime Account

You don't use a phone number to initiate a FaceTime call to someone; you use an email address. The email address connects to that person's use of FaceTime by a FaceTime account.

So to use FaceTime, you must first create your own FaceTime account. The process can be a bit confusing.

You can use an existing Apple ID (recommended) or create a new Apple account for use with FaceTime. If you create a new FaceTime account, it's a new Apple account, separate from your existing Apple ID, or from any other accounts you have. You must use an existing email address, however, for this account.

After you specify your existing Apple ID or create a new account, you then enter one or more email addresses that people can use to reach you on FaceTime. You don't need to include the email address that you used to set up the account as one of the addresses people can reach you on for FaceTime calls.

So, you can get by with a single email address: Use it to set up the new Apple account for FaceTime, and then give it out as your handle for FaceTime calls. But your handle can also be any email address or addresses that you choose.

Before you set up FaceTime, you need to have your iPad 2 connected to Wi-Fi. FaceTime won't work if you're not connected to the Internet, or if you're connected to the Internet using the 3G capability in an iPad 2 Wi-Fi+3G. FaceTime works if you connect to the Internet via a personal Wi-Fi hotspot provided by an iPhone 4, Android phone, MiFi, or other personal Wi-Fi hotspot device.

Follow these steps to set up your FaceTime account.

LET ME TRY IT

Setting Up Your FaceTime Account

1. On the iPad Home screen, tap the FaceTime icon to open FaceTime.

   The sign-in screen appears, with the current image from the front-facing camera in the background, as shown in Figure 13.2. You can complete the rest of this process while looking at a live image of yourself completing the rest of this process!

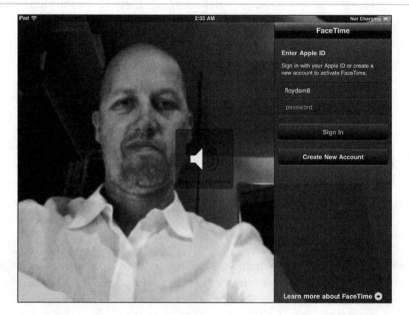

Figure 13.2 *Signing up for FaceTime makes you take a good look at yourself.*

2. To learn more about FaceTime and the iPad 2, click the link, Learn More About FaceTime. To return to FaceTime, double-tap the Home button; then choose FaceTime from among the available apps.

   If you click the link, a Web page with information about FaceTime and other built-in apps for the iPad 2 appears. If you want to view the Web page later, here's the URL: www.apple.com/ipad/built-in-apps/facetime.html.

3. To use an existing Apple ID (recommended), enter the Apple ID and your password. Tap the Sign In button. Skip ahead to step 5.

   A screen appears asking for an email address to use with the account.

4. To create a new account, tap the Create New Account button. Enter your information in the screen that appears, as shown in Figure 13.3. Tap Next and then complete the process to create the account.

   Your account is created. A screen appears asking for an email address to use with the account.

5. Enter an email address that you want people to use to contact you on FaceTime. Reply to the email message that Apple sends you for confirmation.

   Your contacts for the email address you entered appear.

   You have the opportunity to enter additional email addresses if you'd like. You are wise to enter all your email addresses to prevent confusion for people trying to reach you on FaceTime.

   There is apparently a bug at this writing that prevents you from using the same email address that belongs to the Apple ID that you used to create the account at this step in the process. If you try to do so and receive an error message, use a different email account. You can use a friend's email account to help you for confirmation and then delete it later to get around this hassle.

6. To add a contact, tap +. Enter the contact information.

   You can connect with iPhone 4 users on FaceTime by using the phone number assigned to their iPhone 4. Include the complete number—country code and area code. For instance, in the United States, enter the number in this form: +1 (415) 555-1212.

Remember that you can use multiple email addresses associated with your handle. To enter an additional email address for people to use to reach you via FaceTime, see the next section.

Managing Your FaceTime Account

You can do a few things to manage your FaceTime account:

- **Add and delete email addresses:** You can add and delete email addresses that people can use to contact you via FaceTime.

- **Sign Out:** You don't ever need to sign out of FaceTime. If you do, though, you can't receive FaceTime calls.

- **Turn off FaceTime:** You can turn FaceTime off to prevent receiving FaceTime calls.

Here are some steps you can use to manage your FaceTime account.

LET ME TRY IT

Setting Up Your FaceTime Account

1. On the iPad Home screen, tap Settings.

2. Tap FaceTime. The FaceTime Settings screen appears.

3. To turn FaceTime off, drag the slider to the Off position. To turn it on again, drag the slider to the On position.

4. To change your account, tap the Account button. Options appear, as shown in Figure 13.3. Use the options to change your location (what country you're in); to view account details; or to sign out of FaceTime.

   If you sign out, it has the same effect as turning FaceTime off, as described in the previous step.

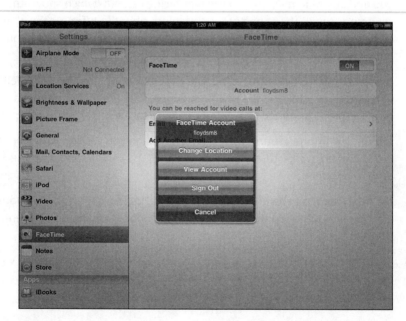

Figure 13.3 *FaceTime has account settings on top of its few other settings.*

5. To add additional emails, tap the Add Another Email button. Type in the email address.

   A confirmation email will be sent to the email address you enter. To enable the email address, follow the instructions in the email message.

6. To delete an email address, tap the email address. Then tap Remove This Email. The email address will be removed.

SHOW ME   Media 13.2—Creating Your Account
Access this video file through your registered Web Edition at
my.safaribooksonline.com/9780132709590/media
or on the DVD for print books.

Making a FaceTime Call

You make a FaceTime call by opening FaceTime and going to your Contacts. You then tap the email address (for a Mac user or iPad 2 user) or phone number (for an iPhone 4 user). You can call the same person again by using the Recents list within FaceTime. You can call a favorite contact by using the Favorites list within FaceTime.

While talking in FaceTime, you can do several things:

- **Switch cameras:** You can switch from the front-facing camera (which shows you and anything near you) to the rear-facing camera (which shows the surrounding scene). This is one of the fun things about FaceTime—the ability to show your surroundings, friends you're with, and so on to the person you talk to.

- **Mute the microphone:** You can mute the microphone during the video call. You can't directly cancel the image, though. (You can switch to the rear-facing camera, or switch to a different app to take yourself out of the picture.)

- **Move your image around onscreen:** The image you send to your call partner shows up as a picture-in-picture window. You can tap and drag this around onscreen.

- **Do other stuff on the iPad:** You can tap the Home button once to choose any app or double-tap the Home button to choose from among currently running apps.

- **Change orientation:** You can also change the orientation of the iPad while using either camera by turning the device. Use the screen lock to prevent the image from rotating as you turn the device.

Follow these steps to make a FaceTime call.

 LET ME TRY IT

Making a FaceTime Call

1. Open FaceTime.

2. To call a Favorite, tap Favorites, and then tap a name in the list.

3. To call a person you recently called, tap Recents, and then choose a name or number.

4. To call a contact, tap Contacts. Choose a name, and then tap an email address or phone number that the contact uses with FaceTime.

5. To add a contact, tap +. Enter contact information, including an email address or phone number that the contact uses with FaceTime. FaceTime initiates the call. If the other party answers, the call begins.

After a FaceTime call has begun, there are several additional things you can do.

LET ME TRY IT

During a FaceTime Call

1. To switch cameras, tap the Camera icon, as shown in Figure 13.4.

   The camera view changes from the front-facing camera to the rear-facing camera, or vice versa.

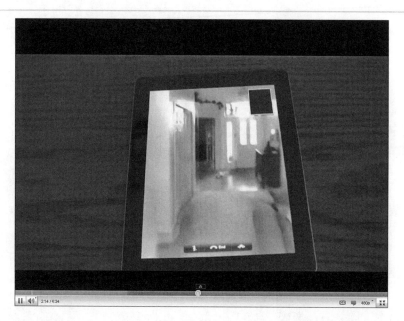

Figure 13.4 *You can switch views or mute the microphone during a FaceTime call.*

2. To mute the microphone, tap the Microphone button. To turn the microphone back on, tap the Microphone button again.

   Audio from you is muted or resumed.

3. To move your own image around onscreen, tap and drag the image around on the screen.

4. To use a different app (and cancel the video feed from you), tap Home and choose any app. Or double-tap Home and choose from among currently running apps.

   The app starts; the FaceTime call continues, but with audio only.

5. To change the orientation of video, turn the device.

   Use the screen lock to prevent the image from rotating as you turn the device.

6. To end the call, tap the End button.

In this chapter you learn how to take photos and videos on the iPad 2. You learn when to use, and when not to use, the iPad 2's cameras versus other types of cameras. You then learn how to take photos and create video clips.

14

Taking Photos and Creating Videos

Taking photos and creating video clips can be a big part of your use of the iPad 2. However, the cameras on the iPad 2 are designed for use with video; using them for photos gives mediocre results when compared to a digital camera, or even many cell phone cameras. Making video clips, on the other hand, usually gives good results. The iPad 2 is especially handy for recording yourself talking about, well, almost anything you want to talk about. Many people like to post such videos, a trend called vlogging or video blogging.

You can use both the original iPad and the newer iPad 2 to get pictures or movie clips created using other cameras, either through syncing with iTunes, as email attachments, or (for photos only) as screenshots from the device's own screen. You can then use your iPad as a truly excellent digital photo frame.

This chapter, however, is exclusively about what you can only do with the iPad 2: creating photos and video clips using the built-in cameras.

iPad 2-created photos and videos show off some of the iPad features present on the original iPad as well. Both iPads are great as photo frames or video frames. From the early days of the iPad, photographers bought an iPad, or several, and scattered them around their homes and studios displaying their work.

The iPad may be the best way ever to show off family photos, vacation snapshots, and images for use at work. The large, bright screen of the iPad, and the simple management tools in the Photos app, enable the iPad to work well as a photo or video frame.

Only the newer version, the iPad 2, has cameras. The iPad 2 has a low-resolution front-facing camera (rated at 0.3Mpx) that's mainly for streaming a live image of you, the user, during a video phone call. It also has a rear-facing camera, which is not quite as low-resolution (0.7Mpx), for streaming the local scenery during a video phone call or for taking pictures.

The only difference with photos on the iPad 2 versus the original iPad is that on the iPad 2 you can take a photo and capture a video clip. The way you manage photos and videos when you get them—whether it's via iTunes, as an email attachment, or by taking them yourself on the iPad 2—is the same on both versions of the iPad.

◉ *Managing photos and videos are covered respectively in Chapter 15, "Importing and Viewing Photos," and Chapter 16, "Importing and Viewing Video Clips."*

 TELL ME MORE   Media 14.1—Why the iPad 2 Cameras Are Low-Resolution

Access this audio recording through your registered Web Edition at ***my.safaribooksonline.com/9780132709590/media*** *or on the DVD for print books.*

Using the iPad 2 to Create Photos and Video Clips

It can take a moment to know whether you have an iPad 2—the device itself has "iPad" written on it. However, there's not a numeral "2" anywhere on the device or in the operating software or apps. The iPad 2 is thinner and lighter than the original iPad, but you can know this if you've had a chance to spend time with both of them.

The key giveaway is the cameras. The iPad 2 has a tiny dimple on the top edge, in the center, for the front-facing camera. It also has a larger hole on the back, in the upper left, for the rear-facing camera. Also, if you look on the Home screen, you see the FaceTime icon. FaceTime is Apple's videoconferencing software.

If you don't have the cameras and FaceTime, then you have an original iPad, not an iPad 2. Please skip ahead to the next chapter, unless you want to learn about using the cameras on the iPad 2.

If you're interested, here's some math relating to camera resolution. The iPad's screen resolution is 1024 x 768, and it takes 3 bytes of computer storage (24 bits) to store full-color information for each pixel. So it takes more than 2MB of resolution to capture a full-resolution, full-color, uncompressed image sufficient to fill the iPad's screen. (After capture, the image can safely be compressed quite a bit, but you need the resolution to begin with to have a good starting point.) The rear-facing camera has only about one-third of that, 0.7MPx, so images are blurry in the background. And you need 2MPx just for screen display. For prints, photo printers typically work at 300 dots per inch (dpi) for low quality, or 600 dpi or more for high quality. At 300 dpi, a 1024 x 768 image is only about 3" x 2.5" in size. For a good-looking, full-size 4" x 6" print, you need much more resolution, up to about 8MPx. Good cameras do some compression as they capture images, so even a 5MPx camera can produce high-quality prints, even at 600 dpi. But a 2Mpx or 3Mpx camera can have visible problems when it's used to produce full-size, 4" x 6" prints. The iPad 2's cameras, at 0.7MPx and 0.3Mpx, respectively, produce poor full-size prints.

The cameras on the iPad 2 are low-resolution cameras that mostly support Apple's FaceTime videoconferencing software. The cameras produce "good enough" images that look fine—and don't take up too much network bandwidth—when streamed at 30 frames per second as part of a video phone call, or saved and played back as part of a movie clip.

There's somewhat of a problem, though, with using the cameras for still photos. You can certainly use the iPad 2 to take photos, and this section explains how to do it. The cameras, though, are not very good for that purpose.

The rear-facing camera is used for video shots of your surroundings during a FaceTime call and for making movie clips and for photographs. When used for video, the camera resolution is given as 720p. This means 1280 x 720, which is in the 16:9 ratio favored for wide-screen display of movies. This would be a 0.9MPx camera if used, without change, for stills.

However, for still images, the edges of the image are cut off to give a blockier, 4:3 ratio, with a resolution on only 960 x 720. That produces images a bit smaller than the iPad's screen (1024 x 768, for both the original iPad and the iPad 2.)

The image that you see onscreen when you take a photo, using the iPad 2 screen as a viewfinder, is a little better than the image that you're likely to get when you take the photo. (The photo may be blurrier, unless your hands are quite steady.) Figure 14.1 shows using the iPad 2 as a viewfinder.

 SHOW ME   Media 14.2—Framing a Photo with iPad 2
Access this video file through your registered Web Edition at
my.safaribooksonline.com/9780132709590/media
or on the DVD for print books.

Figure 14.1   *The iPad 2 screen makes for a bright, large viewfinder.*

The rear-facing camera, when used for stills, is described as having 0.7MPx resolution. That means that an image from the camera has well under 1 million pixels (which is 1MPx resolution). Typical cameras on mobile phones today range from 2MPx on the low end, to 5MPx on the new iPhone 4 (and some mid-range digital cameras), to even higher resolution on some phones and on high-end digital cameras.

The front-facing camera is used for streaming your image during video calls. It deliberately has low resolution, 640 x 480, so that its images are small enough to be streamed at 30 frames per second without using too much network bandwidth.

The resolution of the front-facing camera is described as 0.3MPx, less than half that of the rear-facing camera. Even so, such images, uncompressed, would take up nearly 30MB per second of network bandwidth.

Following is a brief breakdown of the different photo resolutions:

- **0.3MPx (front-facing camera):** A photo that looks grainy onscreen and awful when printed

- **0.7Mpx (rear-facing camera):** A photo that looks better onscreen but still bad when printed

- **1–r2 MPx:** Photos that look good onscreen but usually have visible problems when printed

- **4–r5Mpx:** Photos that look great onscreen and good when printed

- **More than 5MPx:** Photos that look great onscreen and good to great when printed

So the iPad's cameras are, respectively, about one-sixth and about one-third of the resolution, 2MPx, that today is considered the bare minimum for a photograph that looks good onscreen and, with luck, barely acceptable when printed.

For videos, however, the picture is much better (no pun intended). Because videos are created by showing still pictures in rapid succession—a respectable 30 frames per second (30 fps) for iPad 2 movie clips—the eye tends to smooth out rough edges in any one image by blending it with the preceding and following images, producing a relatively attractive image even from fairly rough originals.

In a moving image, the eye can't linger for long on an obscure area or take the time to try to read a street sign in the far background. Motion, especially of people or other subjects, in the foreground tends to take up the viewer's attention. The eye is more forgiving because motion is so interesting.

In addition, although people try to print digital images—often with poor results, compared to what the same image looks like onscreen—they don't expect to print movie images. So the whole "oh no" factor that people can experience when they try to print a digital image is completely missing for digital video.

The iPad 2 still isn't perfect for videos by a long shot. But it doesn't have the under-lying problem with low resolution for video in the same way that it does for still images.

Using the iPad 2 for Photos

When you understand what iPad 2 photos are likely to be good for, and not to be good for, you can have a lot of fun with them. Experiment to your heart's content—just don't bring an iPad 2 as your only camera to your best friend's wedding, unless you really, really know what you're doing.

Ten Things to Know About iPad 2 Photos

Following are the top 10 things you should keep in mind about photos that you take with the iPad 2 cameras, focusing—again no pun intended—on the rear-facing camera that you use for most photographs:

1. **Low resolution:** The rear-facing camera has 0.7Mpx resolution (960 x 720); the front-facing camera has 0.3MPx resolution (640 x 480). This means that pictures tend to be dark, lack detail, and become blurry with motion (by you, as you take the picture, or the subject).

2. **Big, accurate viewfinder:** The iPad 2 screen serves as a big viewfinder that quite accurately reflects the images you get—except the viewfinder images tend to be somewhat sharper and crisper because there's no shutter lag time (which enables blurring) and because you see the images in motion.

3. **Images tend to be blurry:** Unless you have a fairly still subject and a steady hand—from the moment you press the Shutter button until the image Preview icon appears onscreen—the image tends to be blurry compared to what you see onscreen. Even a rock-solid shot tends to be better-focused in the foreground and blurry farther away and in the background. See Figures 14.2 and 14.3 for a "quick and dirty" photo, and the same shot with the photographer's hand steadied.

Figure 14.2 *Taking a "quick and dirty" picture can lead a blurry result.*

Figure 14.3 *Leaning against a wall or leaning your elbows on a table yields better results.*

 SHOW ME   Media 14.3—Steady as You Go
Access this video file through your registered Web Edition at
my.safaribooksonline.com/9780132709590/media
or on the DVD for print books.

4. **OK for onscreen display:** Pictures look decent onscreen, partly because onscreen images are low-resolution and partly because they're brightened by being shown on a glowing screen. Even onscreen, though, they visibly lack detail, especially in far-away and background parts of the image.

5. **Poor print quality:** When printed, though, rear-facing camera images are only about 3" x 3" at 300 dpi (low-resolution printing) and 1.5" x 1" at 600 dpi (mid-range resolution printing.) Images look dark because they depend on reflected light rather than the backlight a screen provides. If you stretch the images to fill, say, a 4" x 6" photo print, they look particularly blurry and dark.

6. **Digital zoom:** The iPad 2 supports up to 5X digital zoom; however, if you use digital zoom, the resulting pictures are even lower-resolution than nonzoomed photos. The more you zoom in, the lower the resolution— the resulting photo appears darker and blurrier as you zoom in further.

7. **Exposure control:** On the iPad 2 screen, when preparing to take a picture, tap the part of the image that you want to use to set the exposure; then watch the image change to reflect your choice. Tap again to use a different spot. (This is exposure control, not focus control as on some cameras.)

8. **No flash:** The iPad 2 doesn't have a flash, front-facing nor rear-facing. If you like taking iPad 2 photos, you may want to consider carrying a hand flash with you, if you can juggle them both.

9. **Neither autofocus nor focus control:** The iPad 2 camera's focus is fixed—it doesn't adjust automatically to your subject, and you can't manually change it.

10. **Great for display on your iPad:** The best way to display an iPad 2 picture is on an iPad, with its big, bright display that's almost the same resolution as the image. The photos also look good on mobile phone screens. On a computer screen, which tends to be darker and larger, more problems are visible—and in print, problems tend to obscure your intent in taking the photo.

11. **And a bonus:** The iPad 2 allows you to edit photos, right on the device. Just tap the Edit button when viewing a photo to bring up options for editing the photo—Rotate, Enhance, Red-Eye removal, or Crop the photo. For more on these options, see Chapter 15.

Understanding When to Use iPad 2 Photos

Photographers have an old saying: "The best camera is the one you have when you need it." The iPad 2 can often be handy for you to take a photo with.

However, you're quite likely to have a better camera, the one on your cell phone, even handier. There's another reason to use the iPad 2, though: It's convenient to have the image right there on your iPad 2 after you take it.

Things you can do with a picture on the iPad 2 include the following:

- **Attach it:** You can attach an iPad 2 photo to an email, tweet, or Facebook posting. This might be your top use for iPad 2 photos for a quick, here's-where-I-am type image.

- **Edit it:** You can use one of the many cool photo apps emerging for the iPad (which work the same on both the original iPad and the iPad 2) to edit the photo. You want to use high-resolution images with a photo app when you can—the saying, "garbage in, garbage out," applies—but it can be helpful to get an image straight onto the iPad 2 for use with an app.

- **Show it off:** As soon as you capture an image on the iPad 2, you can show it off, display it in a slideshow on the iPad 2 screen, or use it as a screen saver, as described later in this chapter.

All this also applies to movie clips and the same iPad 2 cameras that take poor-quality photos take quite nice movie clips. See the next chapter for details.

Of course, you can do all these things with photos you bring onto your iPad 2 as well. When do you use the iPad 2 to take a picture?

In two different sets of circumstances: When your iPad 2 is the only camera you have handy; or when the convenience of getting a photo straight onto the iPad 2 offsets the relatively poor image quality and lack of camera features such as a flash, physical zoom, focus control, tripod, and others.

Following are a few good things about the iPad 2 as a camera:

- **Good resolution up close:** If you get close to a brightly lit object, it can look relatively sharp in the photo. The background tends to be a bit fuzzy by contrast. Sometimes this isn't a bad effect.

- **Quick snaps:** The iPad 2 responds quickly to a shutter press and is quickly ready for the next photo. This is nice because the thing is heavy to hold.

- **Big viewfinder:** With the iPad 2's big, bright screen, it's fun to have a giant viewfinder that's the same size as your photo. The highly accurate preview you get can help you make the most of your iPad 2 photos.

- **Looks good on the iPad:** Your iPad 2 photos look especially good when viewed on any iPad.

The iPad 2 is great for well-lit close-ups of something cute, like a child or a dog. If the image is likely to be shown to people on your iPad or on a mobile phone or computer screen—then your results, if you're a bit careful, will be fine.

Taking a Photo

Because of its lack of features, taking a photo with the iPad 2 is simple. You don't have to turn the flash on or off because there isn't one. There are no adjustments for color balance and only a simple one for light intensity. The iPad 2 is, almost literally, a point-and-shoot camera.

That doesn't mean that you can't make your pictures better, though. Following are a few tips to consider:

- **Free your lens:** If the iPad 2 is positioned so that the camera lens is on the lower edge as you're holding the device, rather than the upper edge, it's hard to keep from covering the lens with your hands. Position your iPad 2 so that the Home button is at the bottom of the screen (in portrait mode) or to the right of the screen (in landscape mode). That way, the camera lens is on the upper edge of the iPad 2, away from your hands.

- **Get a clean scene:** It's more likely that the lens is dirty than clean, so find a clean cloth to wipe it with. Remember to clean the lens any time you get ready to take a photo.

- **Steady as she goes:** Even a little bit of shaking messes up a picture, so try to steady yourself. If you can rest your elbows on a table, for instance, or lean on a wall, so much for the better. Hold the iPad steady from before you press the button until just after the photo thumbnail appears.

- **Let there be light:** Light is the #1 requirement for most photographs, especially with a low-resolution camera. Try to arrange for the subject to be as brightly lit as possible. Get the sun or other bright light source behind you, the photographer, and shining straight onto the subject.

- **You zoom:** There actually is a kind of physical zoom for iPad 2 photos. It's called You Zoom and requires you to move closer to, or further from, the subject, to get the composition of the subject and the background correct. Do this before you consider using the resolution-wasting digital zoom.

- **Slow motion:** Consider asking your subject to pose or hold still; any movement can show as further blurriness in an already blurry picture due to the camera's low resolution.

- **Turnabout is fair play:** Hold the iPad sideways (in landscape mode) for wide shots such as landscapes; hold it upright (in portrait mode) for tall shots such as portraits or full-body shots of people.

- **Photos to the rear:** Use the rear-facing camera whenever possible because it has more than double the resolution of the front-facing camera. For photos of yourself, though, or "sneaky snaps" of people behind you, you may end up using the front-facing camera for some images.

- **Play to the display:** Use iPad 2 photos for images that people view onscreen—on a mobile phone, an iPad, or a computer screen. The images could even be better on such a display than some images taken with better cameras. For a printed photo, or an image that you might want to spend time editing, try to use a better camera.

For a useful gallery of iPad 2 photos, including a few pointers, visit the iPad 2 camera gallery on the CNET website, shown in Figure 14.4. Here's the URL:

http://reviews.cnet.com/2300-3126_7-10007030.html

Figure 14.4 *CNET gave the iPad 2's rear-facing camera a road test.*

Follow these steps to take a photo with the rear-facing camera on the iPad 2.

 LET ME TRY IT

Taking a Photo with the iPad 2

1. On the iPad Home screen, tap the Camera icon to open the Camera app. The current image from the camera appears onscreen.

2. If needed, clean the camera lens. If possible, position yourself with any light source behind you so that the subject is in full light. Move closer or further away, and rotate the iPad 2 to frame the subject appropriately.

3. Check that the still/movie slider is in the still position. If it's not, drag the slider into the still position.

   The slider should be to the left (it's shown to the right in Figure 14.1), and the shutter button should show a camera, rather than a red dot.

4. To switch from the rear-facing camera to the front-facing camera, tap the Switch Cameras icon in the upper-right corner of the screen. To switch back, tap it again.

Use the rear-facing camera whenever possible, because it has more than double the total resolution of the front-facing camera.

5. If you need to use digital zoom, tap the screen to see the digital zoom slider. Drag the slider right and left to compose the shot properly.

    When you use digital zoom, the picture is lower in resolution than when you don't. The picture is more likely to appear blurry and dark.

Figure 14.5 *You can zoom in to frame your subject better, but you lose resolution.*

6. To change the image exposure, tap the part of the image where you want the exposure to be balanced and the image to be clearest.

    If you tap a bright part of the image, it darkens somewhat, and darker parts of the image become darker still. If you tap a dark part of the image, it brightens somewhat, and lighter parts of the image may become washed out due to brightness. See Figures 14.6 and 14.7 for a comparison.

7. Tap the Shutter button, located in the center of the Camera app toolbar at the bottom of the screen. Your iPad takes the picture and then displays a thumbnail version of the photo in the lower-left corner of the screen.

8. Tap the Options button, located in the center of the image, to turn on a grid display. Your screen is divided into nine equally sized rectangles, which you can use to help position your subjects appropriately within the photo.

Figure 14.6   *Here's a photo of computer screens after tapping on the background part of the image to set exposure control.*

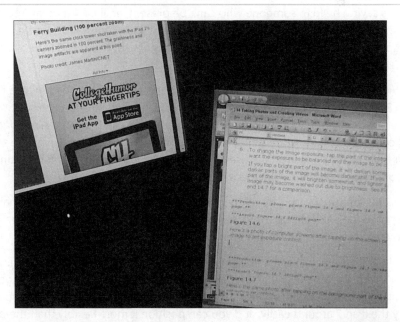

Figure 14.7   *Here's the same photo after tapping on the screen part of the image to set exposure control.*

To see the photo, tap the Preview icon in the lower-left corner of the screen. The iPad opens the Camera Roll, which is where it stores photos you take or bring in from email attachments or from creating screenshots. The Camera Roll displays the photo.

Use Camera Roll to check the lighting, exposure, focus versus blurriness, zoom level (You Zoom, by moving closer or further away, or digital zoom) and other aspects of the photo. Take and compare several photos of the same scene, if possible, to decide which one to keep.

If you can be a bit ruthless about deleting the wrong 'uns right away, you and your family, friends, and coworkers can benefit from the improved appeal of your iPad 2 photo album that results.

Using the iPad 2 for Video Clips

The problems with using the iPad 2 for photos and video clips are complementary mirror images of each other. With photos, lots of people know how to take them well, but the iPad 2's cameras aren't fully up to the task. With videos, the iPad 2's cameras are up to the task, in many ways, but most people don't know how to take them well.

None of this matters for a quick video clip. If you just want to capture a bunch of friends saying hello to someone who can't be present, an iPad 2 is great. You can use the front-facing camera to say hello, the rear-facing camera to capture the group, and then save and send. There are dozens of uses like this one for the iPad 2 camera.

For videos that require more thought, though, there's another use for which the iPad 2 is superior: the webcam-style video so widely used by young people. Young people, who grew up with webcams and digital video cameras on their phones and computers—and who just happen to be naturally fresh-faced and have all their hair—have pioneered the use of webcams for interaction and for creating video messages and how-to videos.

Webcams are usually positioned to look slightly up the user's nose and to make most of us look like ghouls. However, webcam videos have become an accepted form of communication. The iPad 2 is good for them.

A webcam video is just like a FaceTime video call where you explain something, but it's recorded. The iPad 2's front-facing camera is perfect for this. The image is a bit low-resolution, but it's rock-solid, with few dropped frames or artifacts. You can carry the iPad 2 around easily, and you can position it more flexibly than the built-in video cameras found at the top edge of a laptop screen or computer monitor.

The original iPad and the iPad 2 are both widely respected for having excellent battery life. Ten hours is a long time for a device to reliably run on batteries. However, using the iPad 2 for photos and, especially, video, is quite battery-intensive. Also, it can be a less optional use than, say, checking your email; you really don't want your iPad 2 to run out of battery life just as the bride is about to walk down the aisle if you're using it to record a friend's wedding. The fact that you can't swap in a fresh battery for your iPad 2 might become painfully relevant at this point, and many churches and other widely used marriage venues are distressingly lacking in places to plug in your iPad charger. So manage your iPad's battery life carefully if you use it to capture important photos or videos.

Ten Things to Know About iPad 2 Videos

Following are the top 10 things you should keep in mind about videos that you take with the iPad 2 cameras, with equal emphasis on the front-facing and rear-facing cameras:

1. **Low resolution is OK:** The 720p resolution of the rear-facing camera (1280 x 720) and VGA resolution of the front-facing camera are fine for video; in fact, with few dropped frames, either can look good, especially when displayed on an iPad screen.

2. **Big, accurate viewfinder:** You won't find a better video viewfinder than the screen on the iPad 2. What you see is almost exactly what you get on playback, especially if playback is on an iPad 2. This is cool for photos, but it's fantastic for video, where you want to react quickly to changes in the scene.

3. **Weight matters:** Holding an iPad 2 up while you capture a single photo can be difficult. Holding up the device, which weighs about 1.3 pounds, while you capture a school play can be excruciating. There's no convenient tripod attachment either (but third parties have come up with some; see Figure 14.8 for an example).

4. **Great for onscreen display:** Video clips from the iPad 2 look great on iPads and mobile phones. They look quite good on computer monitors as well, although some monitors aren't bright compared to an iPad or mobile phone with the brightness turned up.

5. **Many playback options:** With the appropriate connector, it's easy to use an iPad 2 to drive just about any kind of TV or other video playback device. (See Chapter 1, "Getting to Know Your iPad," for details.) This is a nice-to-have for stills, but it's great for videos.

Figure 14.9 *iPad tripods are here!*

6. **Exposure control:** As with iPad 2 photos, there's exposure control for movies as well. When filming, tap the part of the image that you want to use to set the exposure—then watch the image change to reflect your choice. Tap again to use a different spot. (This is exposure control, not focus control as on some cameras.)

7. **No flash:** The iPad 2 doesn't have a flash. This is a bit less of a problem for videos because motion helps obscure the need to see details, and people don't print video much. As with photos, if you like making iPad 2 videos, you may want to consider carrying a hand flash with you, if you can juggle that and the iPad 2.

8. **No autofocus nor focus control:** The iPad 2 camera's focus is fixed—it doesn't adjust automatically to your subject, and you can't manually change it. This is much worse for movies, where subjects may move about quickly during filming, than for still images.

9. **Shakes less than a phone:** An iPad is less subject to shaking than a phone, which is smaller and therefore subject to the twitches of small muscles. It's easier to hold the iPad steady for a while—but you then have tired big muscles rather than tired small ones.

10. **iMovie available:** Apple has made its iMovie movie editing software available for iPad for the low price of $4.95. This is a bargain and can enable you

to handle basic movie editing quickly and easily right on your iPad 2. (iMovie is deemed too demanding to run on the iPad 1.)

Capturing a Video

For tips and tricks for capturing iPad 2 video, the photo tips given earlier in the chapter are all applicable: Get the lens on the upper edge of the device as you're holding it; clean the lens; figure out how to steady yourself and the camera; zoom by moving closer to or further from the subject (there is no digital zoom for video); get as much light as you can behind you and on the front of the subject; consider asking your subjects to moderate their movements so you can keep up; and target your work for display on the iPad 2.

A couple of the tips for photos are less applicable for movies. You won't often take movies in portrait mode, as people aren't used to that. And you can use the front-facing or rear-facing camera as needed; both produce good results for video playback.

Follow these steps to create a video with the iPad 2.

 LET ME TRY IT

Recording a Video with the iPad 2

1. On the iPad Home screen, tap the Camera icon to open the Camera app. The current image from the camera appears onscreen.

2. If needed, clean the camera lens. If possible, position yourself with any light source behind you so the subject is in full light. Move closer or further away to frame the subject appropriately.

3. Check that the still/movie slider is in the movie position. If it's not, drag the slider into the movie position.

   The slider should be to the right (as it's shown in Figure 14.10), and the shutter button should show a red dot rather than a Camera icon.

4. To switch from the rear-facing camera to the front-facing camera, tap the Switch Cameras icon in the upper-right corner of the screen (refer to Figure 14.9). To switch back, tap it again.

   Use either the rear-facing camera or the front-facing camera as needed.

5. To change the image exposure, tap the part of the image where you want the exposure to be balanced and the image to be clearest.

   By favoring a lighter part of the image, the background may become too dark; if you pick a darker part, lighter areas may become almost too bright to look at. Refer to Figures 14.6 and 14.7 for an example, and then imagine the contrast being continued for part or all of a video clip. Also, be careful about changing the exposure target after you start filming because the change can be disconcerting.

Switch Cameras

Figure 14.10   *Switch from rear-facing to front-facing camera as needed.*

6. To start filming, tap the Record button, located in the center of the Camera app toolbar at the bottom of the screen.

    Your iPad starts recording. If you plan to edit the video, you can continue filming until you're certain that there's nothing you're going to miss—with iMovie and other editing apps, it's easy to cut off unneeded footage after the fact.

7. To stop filming, tap the Record button again. Your iPad stops recording and then displays a thumbnail version of the photo in the lower-left corner of the screen.

To see the video clip, tap the Preview icon in the lower-left corner of the screen. The iPad opens the Camera Roll, which is where it stores videos you take or bring in from email attachments. The Camera Roll displays the video.

Use Camera Roll to check the lighting, exposure, focus versus blurriness, zoom level (You Zoom, by moving closer or further away), and other aspects of the video clip. If you edit the clip, be strict with yourself; a short video is almost always better received than a long one.

In this chapter you learn how to bring photos in from iTunes and email and how to view photos on your iPad. For information about taking photos on the iPad 2, see the previous chapter.

15

Importing and Viewing Photos

The previous two chapters covered topics specific to the iPad 2—using FaceTime and taking photos. Now we return to topics that apply to the original iPad, which doesn't have any cameras and doesn't have FaceTime support, as well as the iPad 2.

One of the great uses of the iPad—either the original, or the iPad 2—is as the world's best photo frame. The iPad's bright, clear screen makes photos look great; its thinness and light weight make it easy to carry around. Many different kinds of iPad stands make the iPad easy to position for showing off photos. (Although you have to think a bit about intermixing photos taken in landscape mode and photos taken in portrait mode.)

From the early days of the iPad, professional and amateur photographers bought an iPad, or several, and scattered them about their homes and studios displaying their work. These people know their equipment. If they think that the best device they can get for showing off their photos is an iPad, I tend to agree with them.

Nonprofessionals use the iPad as perhaps the best way to show off family photos, vacation snapshots, and images for use at work. The large, bright screen of the iPad, and the simple management tools in the Photos app, enable the iPad to work well as a photo frame.

The iPad displays many types of images, including JPEG (most photos), TIFF, GIF, and PNG. For video clips, supported formats include H.264 and MPEG-4 video formats with AAC audio. If you have an image or video clip in a format that the iPad won't display, you can probably find a free or inexpensive converter program online to convert it into an iPad-friendly format.

You can also show photos stored on your iPad on all sorts of displays. If you buy one of the connectors described in Chapter 1, "Getting to Know Your iPad," you can then display your pictures on different types of TVs and monitors. You can also import pictures from a digital camera directly onto an iPad using an optional connector, but you should first import the photos onto your personal computer and then sync the best of them onto the iPad.

One way to get photos onto your iPad, if you have an iPad 2, is by taking them with the iPad itself. (The iPad 2 has a small, but noticeable, camera lens on the back, and a tiny pinhole camera lens in the top middle edge of the front. The original iPad has neither.) Chapter 14, "Taking Photos and Creating Videos," describes taking pictures with your iPad 2.

This chapter describes other ways to get photos onto your iPad 2: by synchronizing your iPad 2 with your personal computer via iTunes, by downloading an email attachment, and by taking a screen shot. (Not a photo exactly, though the screen shot can have a photo on it.)

This chapter also describes how to show off photos on your iPad: by showing them from the Photos app and by using the Picture Frame settings. Using a photo as a screen saver is described in Chapter 2, "Learning iPad Basics." You may want to change your screen saver photo as you get more photos onto your iPad.

The capabilities for managing photos on your iPad include video clips alongside photos. Video clips are generally short videos such as those you might create with the iPad 2 (as detailed in Chapter 14), a webcam, or a digital video camera. I'm referring to them here as video clips to distinguish them from videos, which are TV shows, movies, and other content that you acquire through the iTunes Store. For more information about synchronizing videos, see Chapter 5 "Syncing Your iPad"; for more information about playing back videos and YouTube clips, see the next chapter.

TELL ME MORE   Media 15.1—The Advantages of the iPad for Photos
Access this audio recording through your registered Web Edition at
my.safaribooksonline.com/9780132709590/media
or on the DVD for print books.

Synchronizing Photos

It's fun to keep your latest and greatest photos on your iPad. You can show them off individually or as part of a rotating slide show. You simply create or designate a folder on your computer to synchronize with your iPad. The iPad, unlike the computer, doesn't do multiple windows—it does one thing at a time. Whatever that one thing is takes up the whole screen and looks great.

You should use your personal computer to carefully manage which photos you keep on your iPad; keep the number of photos small and the value of each photo high. That way you can enjoy reviewing and showing off photos on your iPad. A slideshow of your photos on the iPad can be like a greatest hits collection of your photos, plus the current top images.

You don't want any embarrassing or dodgy photos in the slideshow, either—who knows who will see them when you start the slideshow. So use the information given here to help closely manage which photos go onto your iPad.

You can risk emotional pain by not knowing which of your photos stored in various locations are originals and which ones are copies. If you delete a bunch of photos, thinking they're copies, and thereby lose an important original, you could be frustrated indeed. Have a big folder for originals on your personal computer or on a photo-sharing service such as Flickr, and then keep separate folders for "curated" copies—photos that have been selected from larger groups of originals, possibly renamed, and carefully organized into folders. The folder that you sync with your iPad contain only copies, so you can delete items from your iPad, or from the folder on your computer that you sync to your iPad from, without worrying about losing an original.

Follow these steps to synchronize photos from your computer to your iPad.

 LET ME TRY IT

Synchronizing Photos from Your Computer to Your iPad

1. On your computer, arrange the photos you want on your iPad into a specific folder.

   This folder should contain copies of photos that you keep elsewhere—mostly your favorites and new photos that will look great on the iPad.

2. Connect your iPad to your Windows PC or Macintosh. iTunes starts. If the AutoPlay window appears on your Windows PC, use it to upload photos from your iPad to your computer, as described in the next section, or close it.

3. In the iTunes sidebar, click your iPad in the Devices tab. iTunes displays the Summary tab.

4. Click the Photos tab. The Photos tab appears, as shown in Figure 15.1.

SHOW ME   Media 15.2—Synchronizing Photos
Access this video file through your registered Web Edition at
my.safaribooksonline.com/9780132709590/media
or on the DVD for print books.

Figure 15.1   *iTunes makes it easy to sync just the photos you want with your iPad.*

5. Click the Sync Photos From check box to activate it.

6. To synchronize photos from the iPhoto application or Aperture (on a Macintosh only), in the Sync Photos From pop-up menu, select iPhoto. Then select the All Photos, Albums, Events, and Faces option, or select the Selected Photos, Albums, Events, and Faces option, and choose just the items you want. Skip to step 8.

7. To synchronize from a folder on a Windows PC or Macintosh, from the Sync Photos From menu, choose the folder that you want. If the folder you want doesn't appear in the list, click Choose Folder; then select it. Then leave the All Folders option selected, or choose Selected Folders and choose just the folders you want (refer to Figure 15.1).

8. To include video clips in the folder in the synchronization, click the Include videos check box to activate it. Video clips will be included. For more details, see the next chapter.

9. Click Apply. iTunes synchronizes photos between your iPad and your computer.

10. To end the synchronization session after synching is complete, click the Eject icon next to your iPad's name in the iTunes Devices list.

 To save an image attached to an email message, see Chapter 7, "Sending and Receiving Email Messages."

These steps enable you to synchronize photos from your iPad to your Windows PC.

LET ME TRY IT

Synchronizing Photos from Your iPad to Windows

1. On your iPad, delete any photos that you don't want.

    This way you don't have to delete unwanted photos from both devices after you synchronize. Be careful, though—there's no Undo or Recycle Bin to help you rescue your file on the iPad.

2. Connect your iPad to your Windows PC. The AutoPlay window appears, as shown in Figure 15.2.

Figure 15.2   *The AutoPlay dialog can show up so often as to be annoying until you need it.*

3. Click Import Pictures and Videos. Windows displays the Import Pictures and Videos dialog.

4. Optionally, type a tag for the photos, as shown in Figure 15.3.

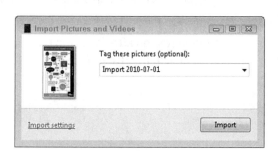

Figure 15.3   *Use the Import Pictures and Videos dialog to import photos.*

5. If you want to delete the photos from your iPad after the import is complete, click the Erase After Importing check box to activate it.

6. Click Import. Your Windows PC imports the photos.

7. After importing is complete, disconnect your iPad from your Windows PC.
    Windows displays the Import Pictures and Videos dialog.

Following are the steps to synchronize photos from your iPad to your Macintosh.

 LET ME TRY IT

Synchronizing Photos from Your iPad to Macintosh

1. On your iPad, delete any photos that you don't want. This way you don't
    need to delete unwanted photos from both devices after you synchronize.
    Be careful, though—there's no Undo or Trash to help you rescue your file
    on the iPad.

2. Connect your iPad to your Macintosh. The iPhoto application opens.

3. In the iPhoto sidebar, click your iPad in the Devices branch. iPhoto displays
    your iPad's photos as Thumbnail icons.

4. Optionally, in the Event Name text box, type a name for the group of photos you're importing. In the Description text box, type a description of the
    event or other occasion.

5. Optionally, click the Autosplit Events After Importing check box to activate
    it and keep events separate.

6. Optionally, click the Hide Photos Already Imported check box to remove previously imported photos from the photos you're viewing and the synchronization process.

7. To import only some photos, click the ones you want to highlight them; click Import Selected. To import all photos, click Select All.

8. When the import is complete, to delete the imported photos from your iPad, click Delete Photos. To leave them there, click Keep Photos.

9. In the iPhoto sidebar, click the Eject icon next to your iPad's name in the Devices list.

Viewing Photos and Videos

After you have photos on your iPad, you can do several things with them. Some capabilities for viewing and organizing your photos depend on your platform:

- **Individually:** You can work with all your photos in one large group. Just look at photo thumbnails and tap to look at a photo.

- **In a slideshow:** For any group of photos, you can start a slideshow. The slideshow can include all the pictures in the group.

- **By album:** Works on any platform. On Windows, albums are simply folders.

- **By event:** Works if you have a Macintosh with iPhoto or Aperture. Photos are organized by event.

- **By face:** Works if you have a Macintosh with iPhoto 09 or later or Aperture. iPhoto identifies faces in your photos and then organizes photos by face.

- **By place:** Your iPad uses the location of photos taken with a GPS-equipped camera, such as the iPhone, or in some cases, the iPad. You can also add the location using certain photo editing programs (called geotagging the photo). Your iPad then organizes geotagged photos by location, which is a surprisingly fun and engaging way to interact with your photos.

Using a Collection

Your iPad's photos are arranged in as many as five different collections: Photos, Albums, Events, Faces, and Places. The Events and Faces categories require that you use iPhoto or Aperture on a Macintosh. Places requires that you take your photos with a GPS-capable camera or use a suitable application to assign a location to a photo. Adding a location to a photograph is called geo-tagging the photo.

All the collections work the same way—you simply open the collection and then view the photos in it—except for Places. With Places, you find a location with photos and/or videos associated with it and then view the photos and/or videos.

These steps allow you to view photos on your iPad.

LET ME TRY IT

Viewing Photos

1. On your iPad, open the Photos app. The Photos app opens, showing the category that you most recently had open and your photos arranged in collections, as shown in Figure 15.4. For Places only, collections are tied to pins on a map, as shown in Figure 15.5.

Figure 15.4   *Your photos show up in collections.*

SHOW ME   Media 15.3—Collections on the Map
Access this video file through your registered Web Edition at
my.safaribooksonline.com/9780132709590/media
or on the DVD for print books.

Figure 15.5   *In Places, collections are tied to pins on a map.*

2. Tap a collection to open it. (This works the same for Places, with its place-based collections, as it does for the other categories.) Use two fingers to spread a collection to preview its pictures; release to leave the collection open, or pinch again to close it.

3. Tap a photo to view it full-screen. Rotate your iPad if needed to best view photos taken in landscape (horizontal) or portrait (vertical) mode.

4. To zoom in on a photo, double-tap it or spread two fingers on the photo. Double-tap again or pinch to zoom back out. Drag to pan. Twist with two fingers on the photo to rotate it onscreen.

5. Swipe to the left or right to see the next or previous photo. Or drag the selection in the row of thumbnails at the bottom of the screen.

    It takes a bit of practice to drag smoothly in the thumbnails, which are small.

6. To delete a photo, tap the photo to see controls, and then look to see if there's a trash can. (Only photos created on an iPad 2, downloaded as an email attachment, or created by a screen grab can be deleted from the iPad.) If there is, tap the trash can to delete the photo; then tap Delete Photo to confirm, as shown in Figure 15.6. To tap photos for which the trash can doesn't appear, delete the photo from the appropriate folder on your computer, and then sync the iPad again, as described earlier in this chapter.

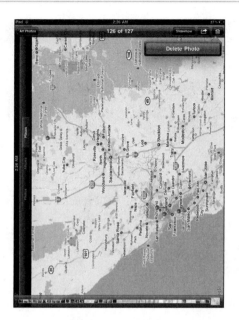

Figure 15.6   *Deleting photos is easy—and permanent.*

The photo is deleted. Keep in mind there's no Undo, and no system trash can where you can go look for deleted items such as photos.

Starting a Slideshow

Starting a slideshow is simple: Just tap any photo in a collection, and then tap Slideshow. The photos in that collection will be used in a slideshow. (Start in the Photos category to use all your photos in a slideshow.) You can choose transitions and music; then start the slideshow.

The slideshow plays only one time. For continuous play, use the Picture Frame option, described in the next section.

Here are the steps to start a slideshow.

 **LET ME TRY IT**

Viewing Photos

1. Open the category and collection you want, as described in the previous set of steps.

2. Tap a photo to view options.

3. Tap Slideshow. Slideshow options appear, as shown in Figure 15.7.

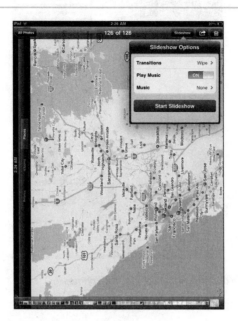

Figure 15.7   *Slideshows are simple and fun.*

Using Photo Options

The Photos app enables you to email a photo and assign it to a contact, as described in Chapter 8, "Managing Contacts on Your iPad." It also enables you to use it as wallpaper, as described in Chapter 2. You might also want to print it and you can if you have an iPad-compatible printer hooked up, as described in Chapter 1. Or you can copy the photo to paste into an app, such as the email app.

Follow these steps to email a photo.

 LET ME TRY IT

Emailing a Photo

1. Open the photo, as previously described in this chapter. Tap the photo options button. Photo options appear, as shown in Figure 15.8.

Figure 15.8 *Photo options let you do a lot with photos.*

2. Tap Email Photo. An email message opens up with the photo pasted in, as shown in Figure 15.8. Note the file size of the image; some recipients have limits on the size of file attachments (though the limit may be quite high, 2MB or more); others aren't allowed to receive messages with attachments.

3. Fill in the To field, the Subject, and the message body. Tap the Send button. The email message with the photo embedded in it is sent. A copy is also sent to your email address.

4. Choose the Transition: Dissolve, Cube, Ripple, Wipe, or Origami. Turn music on or off, and choose your background music from the music on your iPad.

5. Click the Start Slideshow button. The slideshow plays through one time. For some transition options, two pictures may be shown onscreen at one time if there are two vertical pictures and the iPad is horizontal, or vice versa.

6. To repeat, tap the photo to see options; tap the Slideshow button; then tap the Start Slideshow button. The slideshow plays through one time.

Figure 15.9   *It's easy to put photos into emails.*

Showing Photos in Picture Frame

Picture Frame enables you to show photos whenever your iPad screen is locked. You first set up picture frame by specifying transitions and specifying which group of photos (or all photos) will display. This is similar to using the Photos app and creating a slideshow, as described previously in this chapter.

Picture Frame does have an option to zoom in on faces, if you set this up in iPhoto or Aperture, which are only available on the Mac.

You can't have multiple Picture Frame configurations set up. You turn Picture Frame on from the Lock screen, as described in the following steps.

Follow these steps to set up Picture Frame.

LET ME TRY IT

Set Up a Picture Frame

1. Open the Settings app.

2. Tap Picture Frame. The Picture Frame options appear, as shown in Figure 15.10.

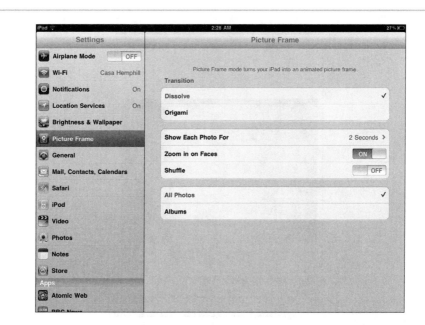

Figure 15.10   *Picture Frame turns your iPad into a photo tour.*

3. Choose the transition; time between photos; whether to zoom in on faces (only if enabled in iPhoto or Aperture on a Macintosh); whether to randomly shuffle images; and whether to use all photos or specific albums.

    The Saved Photos album contains images you've saved on your iPad and are also the only images you can delete directly from the iPad.

Follow these steps to start Picture Frame.

 LET ME TRY IT

Start Picture Frame

1. Lock your iPad by pressing the Sleep/Wake button briefly. The lock screen appears, showing the Picture Frame icon, as shown in Figure 15.11.

2. Press the Picture Frame icon. Picture Frame starts.

3. To pause the slideshow displayed by Picture Frame, tap the screen. The lock screen returns.

4. Press the Picture Frame icon to return to the Picture Frame slideshow, or drag the slider to unlock your iPad.

Figure 15.11 *The Picture Frame icon helps bring your iPad screen to life.*

Editing Photos

The iPad enables you to do a surprising amount of simple editing of photos directly on the iPad:

- **Rotate:** Rotate your photo in 90 degree increments. This is surprisingly useful.

- **Enhance:** The iPad applies a filter to your photo, gently enhancing contrast and bringing out color. You can easily turn on the Enhance feature, see how the results look in your photo, and then revert to the original if you don't like the results.

- **Red-Eye:** Simply tap on each red eye in a photo. The iPad removes the redness.

- **Crop:** The most complicated option, Crop does even more than the name implies. You can easily crop the photo to specific proportions, such as 4 x 6 or 16 x 9; this is called "constraining" the photo. You can also flexibly crop the photo by panning and zooming in and out.

If you zoom into any photo while cropping it, you lose data, making the photo lower-resolution. Photos taken on the iPad 2 are particularly low in resolution, as described in the previous chapter. An iPad 2-captured photo can be fine for a small image online, for instance. But, no matter what the source, if you plan to print a photo, or otherwise need reasonable resolution from it, be sure to test the results of cropping before committing to use a cropped photo.

 **LET ME TRY IT**

Cropping a Photo

Follow these steps to crop a photo:

1. Open the photo, as previously described in this chapter. Tap the Edit button. Photo options appear.

2. Tap Crop. The photo appears in a cropping-ready grid.

3. To change the photo proportions as part of cropping, tap Constrain. Constraint options appear: Original, Square, 3 x 2, 3 x 5, 4 x 3, 4 x 6, 5 x 7, 8 x 10, and 16 x 9, as shown in Figure 15.12. Tap the option you want, and markers will appear onscreen to show the edges of the appropriate cropping area

4. Pinch in and out to zoom into the photo to the right degree. Drag the photo to pan it.

5. To crop the photo, tap Crop. The photo resizes to show what the final result will be. Tap Save to save the result.

   The Photo app will allow you to revert to the original if you need to later.

Figure 15.12 *Constraining a photo crops the edges to a specific ratio*

In this chapter you learn how to bring video clips into your iPad by syncing through iTunes, how to view videos on your iPad, and how to upload videos to your computer and YouTube.

16

Importing and Viewing Video Clips

The iPad is such a great picture viewer that its capabilities as a video viewer are sometimes overlooked. You can use it to buy TV shows and movies through the iTunes Store and download them to your iPad. You can also use the iPad 2 to create video clips, and you can use either kind of iPad to import video clips by syncing with iTunes and to send video clips to YouTube or back to your personal computer.

    ⓒ *For information about buying videos through iTunes and managing them, see Chapter 12, "Managing Music on Your iPad". For information about creating video clips using the iPad 2, see Chapter 14. "Taking Photos and Creating Videos."*

Although the iPad is a great photo frame, it's also a great "video frame"—a device for playing back and showing off video clips. Having so much video power in your hands is a real pleasure. You may see video in a whole new way—no pun intended.

The iPad displays video clips stored in H.264 and MPEG-4 video formats with AAC audio—formats used by many camcorders and video editing programs. Unfortunately there are, at this writing, some relatively common formats for camcorders and so on that just don't work with the iPad. If you have a video clip in such a format, you may convert it in a video editing program or find a free or inexpensive converter program online that can convert the video clip into an iPad-friendly format.

As with photos, you can also show video clips stored on your iPad on all sorts of external displays. With an optional external connector, you can display your pictures on different types of TVs and monitors. You can also import video clips, just like pictures, from a digital camera directly onto an iPad using an optional connector.

However, you can first import the video clips onto your personal computer, possibly edit and compress them, and then sync the best of them onto the iPad.

This chapter describes getting video clips onto your iPad 2 by synchronizing it with your personal computer via iTunes. You can't send video clips to your iPad by downloading a video sent as an email attachment.

The iPad handles two kinds of video. The first kind is referred to here as video clips: home-made videos that you or others create, using a camcorder, mobile phone, or iPad 2. These video clips are stored right alongside photos in the Photos app, as described here and in the previous chapter. The other kind of video consists of TV shows, movies, and other high-value content, which you buy in the iTunes Store. Confusingly, but usefully, you can also buy and rent TV shows and movies of this type through online services such as Hulu and Netflix, which are not covered in detail in this book.

TELL ME MORE   Media 16.1—The Advantages of the iPad for Showing Video Clips

Access this audio recording through your registered Web Edition at my.safaribooksonline.com/9780132709590/media or on the DVD for print books.

Synchronizing Video Clips

As with photos, you can easily keep your latest and greatest video clips on your iPad, watch them, and show them to others. Simply include them with the photos that you sync to your iPad, as described in the previous chapter.

Keep an overall folder on your computer of photos and video clips that you intend to synchronize with your iPad. Keep photos in one overall subfolder at the top level and keep video clips in another. That way you don't intermix video clips—which don't work with slideshows and the Picture Frame functionality—with photos, which work great for both those purposes.

When you show people what you have on your iPad, you're also more likely to want to deal with photos and videos separately. You want to flick through photos quickly, whereas with videos, you may want to take a little more time. Having them separated helps this.

Do as much movie editing as possible on your computer rather than the iPad. Apple is so enthusiastic about video editing on the iPad that it ported its iMovie software to an app, available for the iPad 2 only, as shown in Figure 16.1.

Figure 16.1   *iMovie for iPad 2 enables you edit video clips by hand.*

SHOW ME   Media 16.2—Synchronizing Videos
Access this video file through your registered Web Edition at
my.safaribooksonline.com/9780132709590/media
or on the DVD for print books.

The iPad 2 is somewhat more powerful than its predecessor and can capture video, so iMovie is recommended only for the iPad 2, not the original iPad. It's cool that iMovie is available for the iPad, but it's also cool to have multiple overlapping windows handy on a big screen while you're editing video. And it's really cool to have the much larger storage space of your computer available for different versions of a video clip, for an unedited master copy, and so on.

Consider buying and using iMovie for "quick and dirty" video editing on your iPad 2 and do as much video editing and storage as possible on your personal computer instead. Use your iPad as a kind of video photo frame for video clips that you love and want to share with others.

Also as with photos, you don't want any highly personal, embarrassing, or dodgy video clips on your iPad. People who would never touch your laptop somehow feel quite comfortable picking up your iPad and messing around with it, or looking over your shoulder as you putter around on it. Also it's easy to forget just what's in a given video clip. So it can be good practice to keep it clean and upbeat.

Also as with photos, keep only copies of previously edited video clips on your iPad and in your iPad synchronization folder on your personal computer. The originals are too precious to risk losing in the blur of synchronizing and deleting video clips that may take up too much space on your iPad.

And finally, notice that most of the instructions for video clips in this chapter are quite similar to the steps for photos in the previous chapter. This reflects that iTunes and the iPad manage them right alongside each other. Some different considerations for photos and video clips, though, make it worth spelling out the steps separately.

Follow these steps to synchronize video clips from your computer to your iPad.

 LET ME TRY IT

Synchronizing Video Clips from Your Computer to Your iPad

1. On your computer, arrange the photos and video clips that you want on your iPad into a specific folder.

    Put video clips in a separate folder of their own at the top level of the synchronization folder. This folder should contain only copies of video clips that you keep elsewhere, not originals. The copies can include favorites that you like to share and new video clips that will look great on the iPad.

2. Connect your iPad to your Windows PC or Macintosh. iTunes starts. If the AutoPlay window appears on your Windows PC, use it to upload video clips from your iPad to your computer, as described in the next section, or close it.

3. In the iTunes sidebar, click your iPad in the Devices tab. iTunes displays the Summary tab.

4. Click the Photos tab, which is also used for video clips. The Photos tab appears, as shown in Figure 16.2.

5. Click the Sync Photos From check box to activate it.

6. To synchronize photos and videos from the iPhoto application or Aperture (on a Macintosh only), select iPhoto in the Sync Photos From pop-up menu. Then select the All Photos, Albums, Events, and Faces option, or select the Selected Photos, Albums, Events, and Faces option, and choose just the items you want. Skip to step 8.

Figure 16.2 *iTunes makes it easy to sync just the photos and video clips you want with your iPad.*

7. To synchronize from a folder on a Windows PC or Macintosh, choose the folder that you want from the Sync Photos From menu. If the folder you want doesn't appear in the list, click Choose Folder; then select it. Then leave the All Folders option selected, or choose Selected Folders, and choose just the folders you want.

8. To include video clips in the folders that you synchronize with, click the Include videos check box to activate it.

Video clips will be included. Check the size of video clips to see how much space they take up. A high-quality video clip can take up to 10MB of storage per minute of video, which means 100 minutes of video takes up a gigabyte—a big share of your iPad's available flash memory. But low-resolution video clips can use more like 1MB per minute of video, about the same as an MP3 music file, so check the file size to see what to expect.

9. Click Apply. iTunes synchronizes photos and, if included, video clips between your iPad and your computer.

10. To end the synchronization session after syncing is complete, click the Eject icon next to your iPad's name in the iTunes Devices list.

🜨 *Unlike photos, you can't download a video clip attached to an email message. For information about downloading a photo attached to an email message, see Chapter 7, "Handling Notifications and Email Messages."*

Follow these steps to synchronize photos and videos from your iPad to your Windows PC.

 LET ME TRY IT

Synchronizing Videos from Your iPad to Windows

1. On your iPad, delete any videos that you don't want. This way you don't have to delete unwanted videos from both devices after you synchronize. Be careful because there are no Undo options.

2. Connect your iPad to your Windows PC. The AutoPlay window appears.

3. Click Import Pictures and Videos. Windows displays the Import Pictures and Videos dialog, as shown in Figure 16.3.

Figure 16.3   *Use the Import Pictures and Videos dialog to do what it says on the tin.*

4. Optionally, type a tag for the photos and videos.

5. If you want to delete the photos and videos from your iPad after the import is complete, click the Erase After Importing check box to activate it.

6. Click Import. Your Windows PC imports the photos and videos.

7. After importing is complete, disconnect your iPad from your Windows PC. Windows displays the Import Pictures and Videos dialog.

Follow these steps to synchronize videos from your iPad to your Macintosh.

 **LET ME TRY IT**

Synchronizing Videos from Your iPad to Macintosh

1. On your iPad, delete any videos that you don't want. This way you don't have to delete unwanted videos from both devices after you synchronize. Be careful because there is no way to undo this.

2. Connect your iPad to your Macintosh. The iPhoto application opens.

3. In the iPhoto sidebar, click your iPad in the Devices branch. iPhoto displays your iPad's photos and videos as thumbnail icons.

4. Optionally, in the Event Name text box, type a name for the group of photos and videos you import. In the Description text box, type a description of the event or other occasion.

5. Optionally, click the Autosplit Events After Importing check box to activate it and keep events separate.

6. Optionally, click the Hide Photos Already Imported check box to remove previously imported photos and videos from the ones you're viewing, and from the synchronization process.

7. To import only some photos and videos, click the ones you want to highlight; then click Import Selected. To import all photos and videos, click Select All.

8. When the import is complete, to delete the imported photos and videos from your iPad, click Delete Photos. To leave them there, click Keep Photos.

9. In the iPhoto sidebar, click the Eject icon next to your iPad's name in the Devices list.

Viewing Photos and Videos

When you have videos on your iPad, you can do several things with them. Some capabilities for viewing and organizing your videos depend on your platform:

- **Individually:** You can work with all your photos and video clips in one large group. Just look at photo and video thumbnails, and tap to look at a photo or video.

- **In a slideshow:** For any group of photos, you can start a slideshow. The slideshow can include all the pictures in the group. However, video clips don't work in slideshows.

- **By album:** This works on any platform. On Windows, albums are simply folders.

- **By event:** This works if you have a Macintosh with iPhoto or Aperture. Photos and videos are organized by event.

- **By face:** You can't organize videos by face, only photos, and only if you have a Macintosh with iPhoto or Aperture.

- **By place:** Your iPad uses the location of videos taken with a GPS-equipped camera that adds GPS information to videos, which is relatively rare. You can also add the location using certain editing programs (called geotagging the video). Your iPad then organizes geotagged videos by location.

SHOW ME   Media 16.3—Showing Collections
Access this video file through your registered Web Edition at
my.safaribooksonline.com/9780132709590/media
or on the DVD for print books.

Using a Collection

Your iPad's photos and video clips are arranged in as many as five different collections: Photos, Albums, Events, Faces (not for video clips), and Places. For the Events and Faces categories, you must use iPhoto or Aperture on a Macintosh. (Faces doesn't work with video clips, only photos.) Places requires that you create your video clips with a GPS-capable camera or use a suitable application to assign a location.

All the collections work the same way—you simply open the collection and then view the photos and videos in it—except for Places. With Places, you look for a location that has photos or videos associated with it.

Follow these steps to view photos and videos on your iPad.

LET ME TRY IT

Viewing Photos and Videos

1. On your iPad, open the Photos app. The Photos app opens, showing the category that you most recently had open and your photos and videos arranged in collections, as shown in Figure 16.4.

   For Places only, collections are tied to pins on a map.

Figure 16.4 *You can see key frames above a video.*

2. Tap a collection to open it. Use two fingers to spread a collection to preview its pictures and moving pictures (video clips); release to leave the collection open, or pinch again to close it.

3. Tap a video to view it full-screen. Rotate your iPad if needed to best view
   videos taken in landscape (horizontal) or portrait (vertical) mode.

4. To zoom in on a photo, spread two fingers on the photo. Pinch to zoom
   back out. Drag to pan. Twist with two fingers on the video to rotate it
   onscreen. Tap in the row of key frames above a video to view it.

5. Swipe to the left or right to see the next or previous photo or video. Or
   drag the selection in the row of thumbnails at the bottom of the screen. It
   takes a bit of practice to drag smoothly in the thumbnails, which are small.

6. To delete a photo or video, tap the photo to see controls; then look to see if
   there's a trash can. (Only videos created on an iPad 2 have a trash can.) If
   there is, tap the trash can to start the process of deleting the photo; then tap
   Delete Video to confirm. To tap photos for which the trash can doesn't
   appear, delete the video from the appropriate folder on your computer; then
   sync the iPad again, as described earlier in this chapter.

You can't start a slideshow with a video, and video clips don't show up in slideshows. In Picture Frame, a video shows up as a white box—not a desirable effect among all your great pictures.

Sending Videos to Email and YouTube

The Photos app enables you to email a video, send it to YouTube, or copy and paste it into an app, such as a video editing app.

Follow these steps to email a video.

 LET ME TRY IT

Emailing a Video

1. Open the video and tap the Video Options button.
   Video options appear, as shown in Figure 16.5.

Figure 16.5 *Video options enable you to do several things with videos.*

2. Tap Email Video. An email message opens up with the video pasted in, as shown in Figure 16.6. You may have a problem with the video size because some recipients have limits on the size of file attachments (though the

limit may be quite high, 2MB or more); others aren't allowed to receive messages with attachments at all. However, there's no way to get the file size of a single video from your iPad.

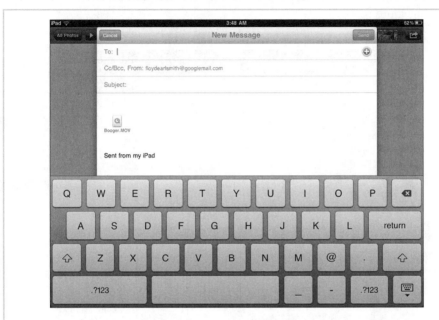

Figure 16.6   *Videos show up as attachments to your email message.*

3. Fill in the To field, the Subject, and the message body. Tap the Send button. The email message with the video attached to it is sent. A copy is also sent to your email address.

You need a YouTube account to send a video to YouTube. If you have a Gmail address, you can use your email address and password to sign in to YouTube. If you don't have a YouTube account or a Google account, you can get one by using the YouTube app on your iPad or visiting the YouTube site with a web browser on your iPad or a personal computer.

Follow these steps to send a video to YouTube.

 LET ME TRY IT

Sending a Video to YouTube

1. Open the video and tap the Video options button. Video options appear.

2. Tap Send to YouTube. A screen appears asking for your YouTube username and password.

3. Enter your username and password, or your Gmail address and password, and press Sign In.

The sign-in pane clears, leaving the Publish Video pane available, as shown in Figure 16.7.

Figure 16.7   *You can easily upload a video to YouTube.*

4. Enter the title and description for the video (both required). The title appears in lists of videos on YouTube. The description appears beneath the video when it's selected to be played.

5. Enter tags for the video (at least one tag is required). The tags are used in searching for the video, so enter tags that describe what's in the video to make searching easier. If your video fits in more than one category (see the next step), you can choose only one, but you can enter the words from one or more others as tags.

6. Tap and choose a category from the rotating wheel. (A choice is required.) Options are Autos & Vehicles; Comedy; Education; Entertainment; Film & Animation; Gaming; How to & Style; Music; News & Politics; Nonprofits & Activism; People & Blogs; Pets & Animals; Science & Technology; Sports; and Travel & Events.

7. Tap to choose the privacy category: Public, Unlisted, or Private. Public videos show up for everyone and can be searched. Unlisted videos are available to anyone with a link but don't show up with search. Private videos are only available to people you specify; you specify who can see the video in your YouTube account on your personal computer.

8. Tap Publish. The video uploads. This can take several minutes. After the video uploads, additional options appear.

9. Tap View on YouTube to open the YouTube app and see the video. Tap Tell a Friend to open an email message with a link to the video on YouTube. Tap Close to close the video and return to the Camera Roll.

If you choose Tell a Friend, you then need to enter the recipient(s) for the message. The message subject is set to the title of the video; edit the subject if needed. The message content is just a link to the video; add to the message content. Tap Send when done.

In this chapter you learn how to use more of the standard apps that populate your iPad and how to get more apps using the famous Apple iTunes App Store.

17

Working with Apps and the App Store

The iPad is a close cousin of the iPhone, and the iPhone introduced the concept of apps—small, focused pieces of code that do a single task well. An iPhone or iPad app is like an application for a personal computer, but it operates under stricter rules, is more focused, and is far easier for users to manage.

The iPhone's apps were originally all from Apple. Developers asked Apple to allow them to create apps, too, and the idea proved to be amazingly popular. Apps are now a huge growth area.

After the iPhone, the iPad is the next logical step in apps. Its bigger screen and greater resources enable apps to do more. It's easier for users to get information from the app and to give input, whether by tapping onscreen or by typing on the onscreen keyboard. So apps are doing more and more.

This is not always good. A home with several children and one iPad may become the setting for constant arguments over who gets it. iPad apps of games such as Angry Birds, Civilization Revolution, and others are surprisingly addictive. And it's easy for any iPad owner to spend a lot of time and money shopping for and buying apps, not all of which get used.

Overall, though, apps on the iPad are a huge improvement over computers and applications for many uses. Simple, focused apps help people get things done so that they then go on to the next thing. The personal computer is still there for in-depth creative work and heavy multitasking, but the iPad often helps people more, while getting in their way less.

This chapter introduces the apps that aren't covered in the rest of this book—YouTube, Notes, and GameCenter. It also describes how to use the App Store to go out and get more apps, the most important single thing you can do to keep your iPad up to date and make it ever more useful with time.

TELL ME MORE   Media 17.1—How Apps Began
Access this audio recording through your registered Web Edition at
my.safaribooksonline.com/9780132709590/media
or on the DVD for print books.

Viewing Videos with YouTube

The YouTube app is a fun part of the iPad and, potentially, a productive part of it as well. While watching a dog ride a skateboard is undoubtedly worth a few minutes of your time, YouTube is also chockfull of videos containing valuable learning and how-to information.

Your iPad is a great way to use YouTube. Its flexibility and convenience make it easy to explore and take in YouTube videos of all types. The long battery life and porta-bility help remove limits.

You can use YouTube only when you connect to the Internet. If your iPad use often takes you out of range of an Internet connection, you should load up on some stored music and videos to fill in the gaps. See Chapter 12, "Managing Music on Your iPad," for more information on how to do that.

It's no accident that the YouTube app works great on the iPad. Until a couple of years ago, YouTube's videos were delivered in Adobe's Flash format, a popular mul-timedia delivery tool. The iPad, though, doesn't support Flash, viewing Flash as too slow and buggy. So YouTube has converted many of its videos to H.264, a format that the iPad does support. The YouTube app plays back only iPad-friendly videos.

If you go out to use videos on websites using Safari (see Chapter 10, "Surfing the Web on Your iPad"), you may run into videos that are still offered only in Flash and don't work on your iPad. If you use the YouTube app as your first resource for online videos, you can reduce your chances of being disappointed by nonworking videos.

Start the YouTube app by tapping it. YouTube opens with a view of several videos, as shown in Figure 17.1.

Figure 17.1 *YouTube offers you several ways into its collection.*

When you use the YouTube app, the millions of videos on YouTube are divided into several channels, plus a few other buttons that help you tame the chaos:

- **Featured:** Tap the Featured button to see videos picked by YouTube's editors. You can see each video's name, runtime, number of views, poster, and approval rating.

- **Top Rated:** This is like the Featured list, but it's ordered by user ratings and views rather than editors' ratings. At the top of the window, you can choose the top-rated videos for today, this week, or all time.

- **Most Viewed:** Again, like Featured, but ordered by the videos that get the most views. A good peek into what appeals most to YouTube users like yourself, this button also lets you choose among the top videos for today, this week, and all time.

- **Favorites:** This is a list of your own bookmarked favorites.

- **Subscriptions:** This one's a list of your video subscriptions.

- **My Videos:** This is a list of videos you've uploaded. It serves as a gentle reminder that you can always contribute to, and look around in YouTube's video library.

- **History:** A list of videos you've viewed.

- **Search:** Every view has a search button to enable you to find videos. You may find that looking at various rankings of the videos gives you ideas for searching for related videos.

You can also watch a video on the YouTube site using Safari. However, the interface is more confusing, and some videos may not work. The YouTube app is the best place to start.

Follow these steps to watch a video in the YouTube app.

 SHOW ME   Media 17.2—Viewing a YouTube Video
Access this video file through your registered Web Edition at
my.safaribooksonline.com/9780132709590/media
or on the DVD for print books.

 LET ME TRY IT

Watching a YouTube Video

1. From the Home screen, tap the YouTube icon to start YouTube.

2. Use the buttons to display different lists of videos. Use the Search function to find videos as well.

3. Tap the video you want to view. The video begins playing. The playback slider shows the video downloading even as the video begins playing.

4. Tap the video during playback to see controls. Controls display, as shown in Figure 17.2.

5. To pause the video, push Pause. (The Pause button changes to a Play button.) To resume, press Play.

6. Drag the scrubbing marker to move forward or backward in the video.

7. Tap the Full-Screen button to enlarge the video to full screen. Tap it again to reduce the size of the video.

8. Tap buttons to Add the video to your favorites; to Share a link to the video in email; to Like or Dislike the video (which serves as a vote on its user rating); or to Flag the video as inappropriate.

9. To leave the video, press Done or Search.

Figure 17.2 *You can control videos during playback.*

Taking Notes with the Notes App

The iPad does many things well, and one of them is taking notes. The Notes app is simple but productive. The simple interface to the Notes app is shown in Figure 17.3.

The Notes app was my own gateway to becoming a frequent user of my iPad. I used to attend community meetings of various kinds and take notes on paper. (A laptop was too big, noisy, and intrusive.) I would then promise people to type up the notes and send them, but about half the time, I never got around to it.

The iPad and the Notes app, however, solved my problem. The iPad is actually smaller than a paper notebook and easy to carry. It's also less obtrusive than a laptop. By taking notes on the iPad, sending the notes out became easy; I just pressed the Email button and sent the notes out on email.

I do joke with people that I've found a $500 solution—that's the cost of a Wi-Fi-only iPad with the minimum 16GB of memory, before tax or accessories—to a $5 problem, which is the cost of a notepad. But the iPad and Notes make a much better solution, and the iPad, of course, does a great deal many other things for me as well.

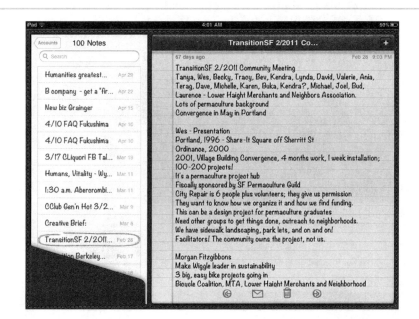

Figure 17.3   *Notes makes it easier to get the most out of your jottings.*

The Notes app is a great way to get to know your iPad. It helps (OK, forces) you to learn to type fairly well using the onscreen keyboard, unless you carry a physical keyboard with you. It also adds value to your iPad by making it home for a repository of important information—the notes that you take.

Try using the Notes app; you may not need a paper notebook.

Many great apps in the App Store are improvements on the built-in apps. (Consider searching on the name of a built-in app and the word "replacement" to start the process of finding such apps.) One of many examples of "upgrades" to existing apps is the pair of popular apps, SoundNote and AudioNote. Both of these apps add sound recording to the Notes app's functionality. You can record a lecture or meeting, for instance, and only type notes to indicate highlights, gestures, the names of attendees, and so on. Notes that you type are keyed to the audio recording's timeline, so you can use notes to move to specific points in the recording.

Notes are stored in order of the date created. The functions available in the Notes app are simple and few:

- **Notes (portrait mode only):** Show or hide the list of previously taken notes.
- **+:** Open a new note.
- **Back and forward:** Move to a previous or subsequent note.
- **Email:** Send the note as an email message to one or more people.
- **Trash:** Delete a note.

> Consider making it a habit to email a copy of your note to yourself so that you have a copy of the note in "the cloud," where it can be searched and isn't subject to loss.

Follow these steps to create a note, email it, and delete it.

 LET ME TRY IT

Writing, Emailing, and Deleting a Note

1. From the Home screen, tap Notes.

2. Tap the plus sign (+) button to create a new note.

3. On the top line, enter the name for the note. Only the first 20 characters or so are reliably visible in the list of notes, so make these first characters meaningful.

4. Enter the body of the note.

5. To email the note, tap the Email icon. An email message opens, as shown in Figure 17.4. The first line of your note is the subject, and the entire note, including the first line, is the body of the email note.

6. Fill in the destination email address; press plus sign (+) to see a list of your contacts and select from the list.

7. Make any needed changes to the subject line and the body. Tap Send to send the note.

   The email message is sent, with a copy to you.

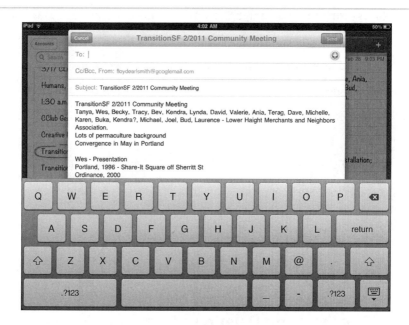

Figure 17.4   *Notes prepopulates most fields of an email message.*

Having Fun with Game Center

The iPad is surprisingly successful as a games platform. It lacks the complicated controllers of other mobile gaming platforms, but that hasn't stopped it from developing its own following.

This is partly because Apple has encouraged developers to make the iPad a gaming controller. The iPad 2 added a faster processor, more flash memory, much faster graphics updating, and a three-axis gyroscope. The new gyroscope makes it easier for games to know just how much the user is moving the iPad 2 and where it's positioned in space. This should encourage the creation of games that take advantage of the iPad in new ways.

Apple's Game Center, shown in Figure 17.5, helps you connect with other gamers. You can make friends with other gamers, team up in multiplayer games, and achieve things and have them noted. For instance, some games use Game Center to host leaderboards, enabling players to compete.

Figure 17.5 *Game Center adds to the iPad gaming experience.*

These steps enable you to create a Game Center account and add a friend.

 LET ME TRY IT

Connect to Game Center

1. From the Home screen, tap Game Center. When you are asked if you want to allow push notifications, tap OK. The Welcome to Game Center screen appears.

2. Enter your iTunes Store account and password; then tap Sign In. Tap Agree to agree to the terms and conditions, and then tap Agree again to confirm.

3. Enter a nickname to identify yourself on Game Center. Tap Next. Game Center displays the Me screen, as shown in Figure 17.6, your reference point for using Game Center.

4. Tap Friends; then tap the plus sign (+) icon to add a friend. The Friend Request screen appears.

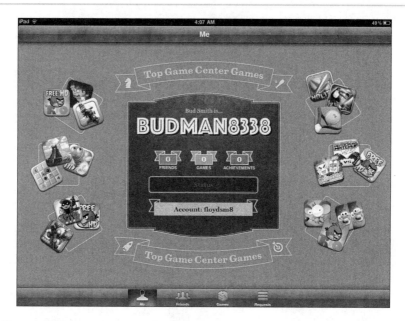

Figure 17.6   *It's all about Me in Game Center.*

5. In the To field, enter an email address or Game Center nickname. Tap Send. Your request is sent. If your request is accepted, the person will be added to your Friends list.

6. Tap OK to finish.

7. To see requests from others, tap Requests. Game Center displays pending friend requests.

8. Tap a request that you want to accept to see details. Tap Accept. Game Center adds the user to your Game Center Friends list.

Rules for Apps to Live By

What makes apps different? Understanding what makes an app different from what came before can help you find the best new apps and get the most out of the apps you have.

Applications for personal computers are often complicated. They have a lot of functionality and often have a long history that affects how they work. Features that made sense back in the Microsoft DOS or Apple II days may not make sense any more but might still hang on as a historical legacy in these days of Windows and the Macintosh.

Because personal computers let you do all sorts of things, it can be easy for using applications to be confusing. Just managing the files that make up an application, plus the data files you create as you use applications, is overwhelming for many people.

The iPad doesn't let you deal directly with files. As a result, apps do their own file management, but they keep it simple. For instance, the Notes app, introduced earlier in this chapter, just has one list of notes you've created, in date order. You might take a little bit of time finding an older note in a long list, but you won't accidentally misfile it someplace where you'll never find it again.

The Notes app just does the basics. If you need something more powerful, replacements abound. But they tend to follow the same overall template as the Notes app.

The App Store also helps. It's a lot like a music store. You decide on whether to buy an app based on a short description or user ratings and not much else. It's not a big problem, though, because apps are so inexpensive—usually less than $5. There have already been billions of dollars made from these low-cost purchases.

Apple approves every app that appears in the App Store and has not always been transparent, or even reasonable, about what it does and doesn't let through. However, overall, Apple's control of the App Store has kept a lot of junk out and contributed to its popularity and profitability.

Now it is possible for an app to get too complex. For instance, Apple's iMovie app inherits a lot of power from its older brother on the Macintosh. It has so much capability that it can take days to find all of it—and it can be hard to find a specific function just when you need it.

Still, apps tend to be simple, just powerful enough, and relatively inexpensive. The App Store can be expected to keep contributing to the success of the iPad, and its cousins the iPhone and iPod Touch, for a long time.

 SHOW ME   Media 17.3—Finding and Installing an App
Access this video file through your registered Web Edition at
my.safaribooksonline.com/9780132709590/media
or on the DVD for print books.

Finding and Installing Apps

Your iPad comes with a set of apps that help you get off to a running start, but there's so much more you can do. The App Store is key to helping you get the most out of your iPad.

You can find great apps and learn more about them in several ways:

- **Through the App Store on your iPad:** This is a simple interface that enables you get straight to apps.

- **Through the App Store in iTunes on your personal computer:** This is a more powerful interface that enables you get more information, both through iTunes running on a larger screen, and by sharing the screen with a Web browser for additional digging.

- **Through reviews, app maker's websites and online comments:** Search online for "best of" lists, reviews of specific types of apps, and information on developer websites. This helps you make the most of the precious time and, in many cases, money you spend on apps.

Use these resources iteratively and interactively, as if you were shopping for something relatively expensive. That way you're more likely to end up with a smaller selection of good apps on your iPad, not just a hodgepodge.

> To get the most out of apps, be selective about what you buy or download for free. Arrange apps in folders on your Home screen so that you can more easily find what you want and delete apps you don't use. And, shop the App Store, search relevant sites, and read articles about top apps to stay up to date on apps that might work for you.

Follow these steps to find and install an app from the iPad.

 **LET ME TRY IT**

Finding and Installing an App from the iPad

1. From the Home screen, tap App Store. The App Store appears, showing Featured apps, as shown in Figure 17.7.

Figure 17.7 *The App Store is the secret to super-charging your iPad.*

2. To see different views on apps, tap New for recent releases, What's Hot for popular apps, and Release Date to see all apps organized by date of release.

3. To use other functions, tap Genius to start an app recommendation service from Apple; tap Top Charts to see the highest-rated apps; tap Categories to see apps in topical groups. Tap Updates to download and install updates for your existing apps.

4. To search for an app, enter keywords in the search box in the upper-right corner; then press Search on the onscreen keyboard. Choose your app from the results that appear.

5. When you see an app that looks good, tap it. Details appear, as shown in Figure 17.8. Take your time to learn more about the app. One clue: Read the comments carefully, especially for mention of competing apps you might also be interested in. Search in Safari, or in a web browser on your computer, for the same thing.

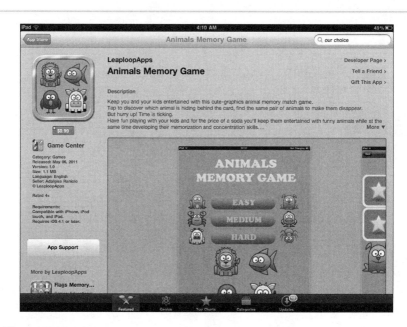

Figure 17.8 *Follow the links to learn more about an app.*

6. To buy an app, tap the button in the upper left that gives the price (such as $4.99 or Free). The button changes to say Buy App if there's a price, or Download App if it's free.

7. Press the button (Buy App or Download App) to confirm.

8. The app is downloaded and installed. Game Center displays pending friend requests.

18

Customizing Your iPad

One of the advantages of using the iPad is its utter simplicity in so many operations. The iPad is "locked down"—not subject to change—to a much greater extent than a personal computer.

However, you may want to make some useful changes. You have your own way to get things done, and you can customize your iPad in several ways to fit your needs. For instance, you not only can move icons around on the Home screen, but you can also create folders and arrange apps into them. You can also change the screen brightness, which is a near-necessity because the brightness level around you changes while you use your iPad.

You can use the customization tools described here to change and improve the way your iPad works for you. This chapter shows you how to use a "top ten" of customization changes for your iPad.

Customizing the Home Screen

The iPad is different from a personal computer in one important way: There are no overlapping windows. Each app you use completely takes over the screen. So the iPad's Home screen is very, very important. You're likely to find yourself frequently returning to the Home screen to start a new app.

There is one feature available on your iPad that comes close to the effect of overlapping windows: using a browser that supports tabs. The built-in Safari browser does not support tabs, but third-party browsers available from the App Store do. Using a tabbed browser on the iPad is a joy.

The Home screen is more than one screen of content. It's made up of six panes, each the size of a full screen, which can hold app icons and folders. Each screen can hold up to 20 icons, with a mix of app icons and folders that can each hold many apps. See Figure 18.1 for an example of one pane.

Figure 18.1   *The Home screen uses up to six panes, with up to 20 icons each.*

   SHOW ME   Media 18.1—Working with Panes on the Home Screen
Access this video file through your registered Web Edition at
my.safaribooksonline.com/9780132709590/media
or on the DVD for print books.

When you press the Home button, you go to the first pane. Swipe the screen to see the next pane to the right, and keep going for up to six panes that are available for app icons and folders.

Every pane shows the Dock, which is populated with four icons when you first get your iPad. (These icons do not also show up on the other part of the Home screen.)

You have three options for customizing the Home screen:

- Move icons around to different panes.

- Create folders and move icons into and out of folders.

- Move icons and folders to and from the Dock that's available at the bottom of each pane of the Home screen.

Arranging your icons and folders on the Home screen is a challenge because you want two contradictory things: You want to keep tweaking the layout so that it works for how you want to use it differently over time; and you want a layout that doesn't change much so that you can develop muscle memory for often-repeated tasks. Keep in mind that a given task can involve using more than one app, such as checking your email and social media apps when you first turn on your iPad in the morning.

So try to put some up-front thought into creating a layout that works for you, and that you can add to over time, without wholesale changes. Start with the Dock. If you can put your six most frequently used apps in the Dock, in a sensible order, you can get to them without much thought.

Then concentrate on the first pane of your Home screen. Put more frequently used apps there, again in a sensible order. You can use folders if you'd like.

Use the remaining panes in a lot of different ways. You can devote panes to themes such as news or sports, depending on your interests. You can do the same thing with folders. Remember that the fewer panes you use, the less swiping around you have to do to find something.

You might find the process to be fun. Following is a detailed description of how to get icons into the Dock; how to move icons around onscreen; and how to create a folder and move icons into it.

Follow these steps to put an icon in the Dock that appears at the bottom of each pane of the Home screen.

 LET ME TRY IT

Putting an Icon in the Dock

1. From the Home screen, swipe to bring up the pane with the icon that you want to put in the Dock.

2. With the desired icon in view, tap and hold any icon until it starts to shimmy. All the icons shimmy. An X appears on each icon that you can delete; don't touch any of the Xs unless you mean to.

3. If there are already six icons in the Dock, drag one out of the Dock onto a pane of the Home screen. This opens up an empty space in the Dock.

4. Drag the desired icon into any desired position in the Dock, as shown in Figure 18.2. Other icons move around to accommodate the new one.

5. Drag the other icons in the Dock around if needed to put them in the desired order.

6. Press the Home button to return the icons to normal status.

Figure 18.2   *If there's room, the Dock icons shift to accept another icon in the Dock.*

The next set of steps enable you to move an icon—either an app icon or a folder icon—around on the Home screen, including from one pane to another.

 SHOW ME   Media 18.2—Putting Icons in the Dock
Access this video file through your registered Web Edition at
my.safaribooksonline.com/9780132709590/media
or on the DVD for print books.

 LET ME TRY IT

Moving Icons Around on the Home Screen

1. From the Home screen, swipe to bring up the pane with the icon that you want to move. You may also want to check the pane or folder that you want to move the icon into to make sure there's room.

2. With the desired icon in view, tap and hold any icon until it starts to shimmy. All the icons shimmy. An X appears on each icon that you can delete; don't touch any of the Xs unless you mean to.

3. To move the icon on the same pane, drag it to the desired spot. Other icons shift to make room for the icon that you're moving.

4. To move the icon to a different pane, drag it to the right or left edge of the current pane—in the direction you want to move the icon. The next pane over on that side replaces the current pane.

5. Continue dragging the icon to the edge of a pane until you reach the pane you want.

6. Place the icon in the desired position in the pane and, if desired, in the folder you want.

7. Press the Home button to return the icons to normal status.

Folders on the iPad home screen are not created in the same way they would be on a personal computer, such as pressing on an empty square to see a New command, or some similar approach. Instead, you create a folder by dragging the icon of one app onto another. Your iPad creates a folder with both icons in it, gives it a name, and gives you the opportunity to rename the folder.

If you want a folder with just one icon in it, create a folder with two icons; then drag one of them out.

Following are the steps to create a folder.

 LET ME TRY IT

Creating a Folder

1. From the Home screen, swipe to bring up the pane with the icon that you want to use to create a folder.

2. With the desired icon in view, tap and hold any icon until it starts to shimmy. All the icons shimmy. An X appears on each icon that you can delete; don't touch any of the Xs unless you mean to.

3. Drag the icon that you want to put in a folder over another icon. Your iPod creates a folder.

4. Release the icon. A folder is created with the two icons in it, as shown in Figure 18.3. Your iPad gives the folder a name according to the category that the app you're dragging belongs to.

5. To rename the folder, tap on the text box with the folder name to bring up the onscreen keyboard. Enter the new name.

6. If you want to remove an icon from the folder, drag it out. You can remove one icon from a folder that has the original two icons in it. But if you also drag the last icon out, the folder disappears.

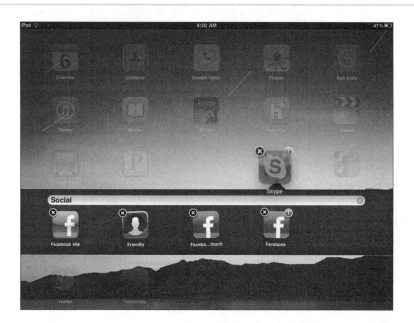

Figure 18.3   *Dragging one icon over another creates a folder.*

7. Tap the folder to close it.

8. Drag additional icons into the folder if you'd like.

9. Press the Home button to return the icons to normal status.

Managing iCloud Settings

You and your iPad have access to iCloud, which provides two major functions:

- Synchronization among zero, one, or more Macintosh computers and one or more iOS devices—iPads, iPhones, and iPod Touch devices on which you access an iCloud account.

- Backup for one or more devices, providing 5GB of free storage for your iPad data. Your iPad has at least 16GB of storage, so you will probably have to be selective in what you back up—or just buy extra iCloud storage and back up more of your data.

To manage use of iCloud on your iPad, you make two sets of choices:

- Which apps and functions to synchronize

- Which apps and functions to back up

 **LET ME TRY IT**

Synchronizing and Backing Up in iCloud

Follow these steps to choose which apps to synchronize and which apps to back up:

1. From the Home screen, tap Settings. The Settings app opens.

2. Tap iCloud. The iCloud Settings screen opens, as shown in Figure 18.4.

Figure 18.4 *Start by choosing which apps to synchronize in iPad.*

3. For each app or function displayed, use the slider to turn synchronization on or off. You might choose to synchronize your calendars across devices, for instance, but not your photos.

4. To set storage and backup options, tap the tab Storage & Backup. The Storage & Backup screen appears.

5. Tap Manage Storage to manage apps. The Manage Storage screen appears.

6. Tap the name of your iPad, labeled This iPad. The Info screen appears, as shown in Figure 18.5.

Figure 18.5 *Choose which apps to back up in iCloud.*

7. For each app, use the slider to back it up in iCloud or not. Tap Show All Apps to show more apps and continue choosing which apps to back up in iCloud.

8. When you're finished, you can exit the iCloud Settings.

9. You can back up immediately by returning to the Storage & Backup screen, ensuring you have Wi-Fi access, and tapping the button, Back Up Now. Your iPad will automatically back up when it's locked and connected to a power source and Wi-Fi.

Putting the iPad in Airplane Mode

Your iPad has several antennas that constantly scan for different types of signals. A Wi-Fi-only iPad has a Bluetooth antenna and one for Wi-Fi connections. A Wi-Fi+3G iPad adds a 3G cellular antenna and a GPS antenna for getting your location.

When you take a plane trip, airline personnel ask you to completely turn off all electronic devices on take-off and landing. Turning off the iPad turns off all the antennas. When you are allowed to turn your iPad back on, though, during a flight, you still need to turn all the antennas off.

To quickly turn off antennas, your iPad provides airplane mode. Use airplane mode to operate your iPad safely while in flight.

On some flights, you may be allowed to connect to Wi-Fi during the flight. In these cases, you should turn on Wi-Fi, but still turn off the other antennas—Bluetooth and, if you have a 3G iPad, 3G and GPS.

Follow these steps to put your iPad in airplane mode.

 LET ME TRY IT

Putting an iPad in Airplane Mode

1. From the Home screen, tap Settings. The Settings app opens.

2. Drag the slider to move the Airplane Mode switch to On. Your iPad disables all antennas and displays an Airplane icon in the upper left of the status bar, as shown in Figure 18.6.

Figure 18.6   *Your iPad shows an Airplane icon to remind you that the Airplane Mode switch is on.*

TELL ME MORE   Media 18.3—Using a Passcode

Access this audio recording through your registered Web Edition at
my.safaribooksonline.com/9780132709590/media
or on the DVD for print books.

Using a Passcode Lock

A passcode lock helps protect you from illicit use of your iPad by others when someone gains access to your iPad, either by borrowing it or by theft. Anyone can turn an iPad on and use it if it's not protected by a passcode lock. Using the passcode lock protects your data, such as your personal email, and prevents people from, for instance, making online purchases with stored passwords and credit card numbers.

You can enter a simple passcode of four digits, like a bank ATM PIN number, or a more complex one:

- **Simple passcode:** A four-digit code that could be vulnerable, with "only" 10,000 possibilities. If it's the same passcode you use for other purposes or is a birthday or something else that could be guessed, it's particularly vulnerable.

- **Complex passcode:** A longer combination of letters, numbers, and symbols, with millions of possibilities. To get the highest passcode strength, combine lowercase letters, uppercase letters, numbers, and symbols. (Yes, this requires you to switch among different onscreen keyboards to enter your passcode!)

If you want to enter a complex passcode, follow the steps in "Protecting Your iPad with a Passcode Lock" exactly as presented. In particular, drag the Simple Passcode slider to Off as a first step—before you tap the Turn Passcode On button, not after. This takes some doing, as the Turn Passcode On button is at the top of the screen, whereas the Simple Passcode slider is well below it, halfway down the screen.

Follow these steps to equip your iPad with a simple or complex passcode.

LET ME TRY IT

Protecting Your iPad with a Passcode Lock

1. From the Home screen, tap Settings. The Settings app opens.

2. Tap Passcode Lock. The Settings app displays the Passcode Lock screen.

3. If you want to enter a complex passcode, drag the Simple Passcode slider in the middle of the screen to Off. Your iPad now enables you to enter a complex passcode.

4. Make sure to review the previous step—then, tap the Turn Passcode On button. Your iPad prompts you to enter a passcode. The entry screen for a complex passcode is shown in Figure 18.7.

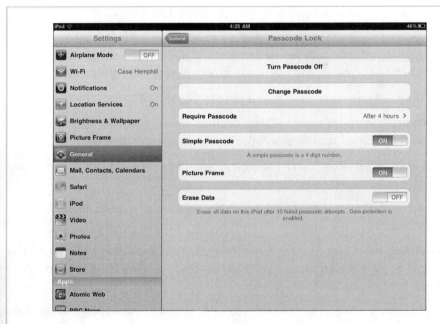

Figure 18.7   *Enter a complex or simple passcode, as your needs dictate.*

5. Carefully tap your passcode. If you enter a complex passcode, tap Next. For a simple passcode, enter four digits. For a complex passcode, consider combining lowercase letters, uppercase letters, numbers, and symbols. Your iPad displays the passcode as dots, so be sure you know, and remember, what characters you enter.

6. Tap your passcode again.

7. If you enter a complex passcode, tap Done. Your iPad is now passcode-protected. Make sure you don't forget your passcode!

Turning on Parental Restrictions

The iPad comes equipped with the capability to use a set of parental restrictions that manage what kind of apps and content people of different ages can access. These restrictions can block some risqué content; however, they are not fully reliable, so you should use other tactics besides parental restrictions to manage what younger people who use your iPad can use it for.

Parental restrictions work with software and content that has an age restriction. When software developers send their apps to Apple for review, they must include a parental restriction rating. Apple must approve the suggested rating before the app can go in the App Store. So software ratings are fairly strong.

However, web pages are often not rated. So a web browser, such as the Safari app built into the iPad, can easily be used to access risqué content and related functionality. Email, Facebook, and Twitter are other avenues for risqué content.

There is a lot of protection built in. You can manage the following:

- **Apps:** Restrictions apply to Safari, YouTube, iTunes, Ping (the Apple social network for iTunes), and whether apps can be installed or deleted.

- **Location Services:** You can turn off location services for apps that use them, such as Maps and Safari.

- **Accounts:** You can disallow the addition, deletion, or modification of accounts.

- **In-App Purchases:** You can turn off the ability to make in-app purchases. This can be a good idea; some apps encourage the spending of up to hundreds of dollars in a single session.

- **Country settings:** You can set the country whose standards are used for ratings.

- **Explicit ratings:** You can disallow music and podcasts with an Explicit rating.

- **Movies:** You can allow or disallow movies based on their ratings—for instance, the Motion Picture Association of America (MPAA) rating in the United States: G, PG, PG-13, R, or NC-17.

- **TV shows:** You can allow or disallow TV shows based on their rating as well; for the United States, ratings are similar to MPAA ratings.

- **Apps:** You can allow or disallow apps based on their ratings: 4+, 9+, 12+, or 17+.

- **Game Center:** You can allow or disallow multiplayer games or adding friends.

So, if you need to protect a younger user from dubious content, do use parental restrictions. Be prepared, however, to do what you can to manage and monitor usage in additional ways as well.

Follow these steps to activate parental restrictions for your iPad.

 LET ME TRY IT

Activating Parental Restrictions

1. From the Home screen, tap Settings, and then tap General. The Settings app displays the General screen.

2. Tap Restrictions. The Restrictions page appears, as shown in Figure 18.8.

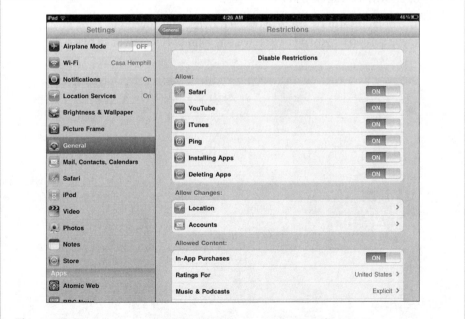

Figure 18.8 *Use parental restrictions to help manage apps and content.*

3. Tap Enable Restrictions. The Settings app displays the Set Passcode screen.

4. Enter the four-digit passcode, as described previously in this chapter; then retype the code. The Settings app returns to the Restrictions screen and turns all controls to On, including Safari, YouTube, and others.

5. To disable restrictions where there's a slider, drag the slider to Off. Sliders control settings for Safari, YouTube, iTunes, Ping, installing and deleting apps, in-app purchases, and Game Center.

6. Tap the Location and Accounts buttons and use the submenus to disable restrictions for location services (for each app that uses them) and for accounts.

   Built-in apps that use locations services include Maps and Safari. Many third-party apps use location services, including Facebook.

7. Tap the Ratings For button to change the country whose ratings standards will be used.

8. Tap the Music & Podcasts button to allow or disallow content rated Explicit.

9. Tap the Movies, TV Shows, and Apps buttons to set ratings for each type of functionality. Tap to set the rating to the highest level you want to allow, as shown (for Movies) in Figure 18.9.

   The default settings are to allow all movies, TV shows, and apps, so change these settings if you want to have any kind of restrictions in place.

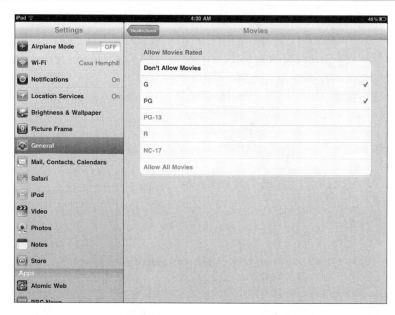

Figure 18.9 *Set ratings for Movies and other types of content.*

Customizing the Wallpaper

Wallpaper is the name for the images that appear in the background for your Home screen and Lock screen. The iPad comes with two rather nice images in place, but you can choose from a total of 30 images that are provided with your iPad, or use your own.

You may want to use an imported image for wallpaper; importing images is described in Chapter 15, "Importing and Viewing Photos." If you have an iPad 2, you may want to use a photo you take with the iPad as a wallpaper image; taking a photo with the iPad 2 is described in Chapter 14, "Taking Photos and Creating Videos."

Follow these steps to change the wallpaper for your iPad's Home screen and Lock screen.

 LET ME TRY IT

Changing the iPad's Wallpaper

1. From the Home screen, tap Settings; then tap Brightness & Wallpaper. The Brightness slider and a button showing the current wallpaper for the Home and Lock screens display.

2. Press the Wallpaper button. A set of containers for images appears, as shown in Figure 18.10: The 30 images that come with your iPad, images you've saved with screen captures or images downloaded as email attachments, and images you've imported from your personal computer.

3. Find the image you like and tap it. The image enlarges to fill the screen, and buttons appear for various options, as shown in Figure 18.11.

4. To use the chosen image for the Lock Screen, tap Set Lock Screen. To use it for the Home Screen, tap Set Home Screen. To use the same image for the Lock Screen and Home Screen, tap Set Both. To go to a different image, press Cancel. The image is used as indicated by the button you choose.

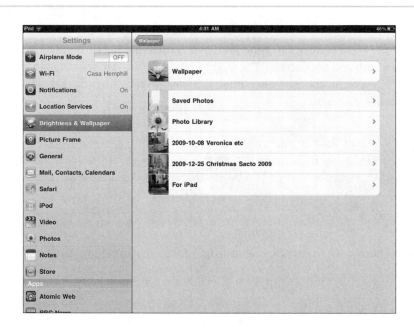

Figure 18.10   *You can choose from any image stored on your iPad for wallpaper.*

Figure 18.11   *The iPad gives you options for the image you choose.*

5. To check how an image looks on the Home screen, press the Home button. To check how an image looks on the Lock screen, press the Sleep/Wake switch to put your iPad to sleep; then press the Sleep/Wake switch again to wake your iPad. To return to the Wallpaper setting, double-press the Home button, choose Settings, Wallpaper.

6. Continue reviewing images and assigning them to the Lock Screen and/or Home Screen until you're happy with the results.

Changing the Screen Brightness

Apple tends to tightly control the interfaces of its consumer electronics devices, such as the iPod Touch, iPhone, and iPad. It takes strong steps to make things simple. Most of the choices Apple makes are admirable; almost all are defensible.

One choice, though, that I have a hard time with is the lack of a physical screen brightness adjustment. The only screen brightness control is a software adjustment in Settings. It's not obvious what an ideal screen brightness control would look like. However, I find the lack of one a real pain.

It's a hassle to leave what you're doing on the iPad to change the brightness—especially as the desired brightness can change with a cloud passing in front of the sun or as you move from one app to another. A few apps have in-app brightness controls to make up for this, but that just adds inconsistency and confusion.

Making it worse, some apps don't remember exactly where you were when you leave the app to do something else. There's a game that I play, Civilization Revolution, that loses the last couple of moves I make when I leave it to do something else. So I have to save and reload the game each time I want to change brightness.

The iPad does have an automatic brightness adjustment setting that uses the ambient light setting on the iPad to change the brightness. Although this is a viable option, it's often noticeably different from what I want at a given time.

If you, too, don't like to use the automatic brightness adjustment—at least not all the time—then you want to get good at changing the screen brightness in Settings, as described here.

Follow these steps to change the screen brightness for your iPad.

LET ME TRY IT

Changing the Screen Brightness

1. From the Home screen, tap Settings; then tap Brightness & Wallpaper. The Brightness slider and a button showing the current wallpaper for the Home and Lock screens display.

2. To change the screen brightness, drag the slider left to dim the screen or right to brighten it.

3. To let your iPad change the screen brightness automatically, using the ambient light sensor, drag the Auto-Brightness slider to On. To have the brightness slider completely control the screen brightness, drag the Auto-Brightness slider to Off.

Turning iPad System Sounds On and Off

The iPad doesn't enable you to use custom sounds for various system functions. It does enable you to turn sounds for these functions on or off and set the volume:

- New Mail
- Sent Mail
- Calendar Alerts
- Lock Sounds
- Keyboard Clicks

By default, all sounds except keyboard clicks are set to Off.

Follow these steps to turn system sounds on and off for your iPad, to preview each sound, and to set the volume for all sounds.

 LET ME TRY IT

Turning System Sounds On and Off

1. From the Home screen, tap Settings; then tap General.

2. Tap the button, Sounds. Sounds options appear, as shown in Figure 18.12.

Figure 18.12 *You can turn on sounds for specific alerts and actions.*

3. Drag the slider to turn sounds on and off for new mail, sent mail, calendar alerts, lock sounds, and keyboard clicks. As you drag a slider to On, the sound clip used for that system function plays, as a preview. By default, only the sound for keyboard clicks is turned on.

4. To set the volume setting for all the sounds, drag the volume slider left (for quieter sound) or right (for louder sound).

   You can't set the volume separately for different sounds—all the sounds that you activate are controlled by a single volume setting.

Adding Keyboards and Changing Settings

Lots of people complain about the iPad's onscreen keyboard at first, and many buy a physical keyboard to speed text entry. However, most people grow accustomed to the onscreen keyboard quickly, and many of those physical keyboards end up going more or less unused.

There are two entirely different sets of keyboard options for the iPad, which are, perhaps unfortunately, combined in one group of settings. The first controls how much the keyboard interferes with the exact characters you type. These settings include the following:

- **Auto-Capitalization:** The iPad can capitalize the first letter of a new sentence for you automatically, unless you turn the option off.

- **Auto-Correction:** The iPad can fix your mistakes, but can also convert many unusual but correct words, acronyms, and so on into whatever it "thinks" you should be typing. Again, you can turn this off.

- **Check Spelling:** The iPad can check your spelling, helping you sometimes and just being dense others, unless you turn the option off.

- **Enable Caps Lock:** The iPad has a caps lock key, but for some reason it's turned off by default when you get a new iPad. Come to this screen to turn it on.

- **"." Shortcut:** This is one of the more useful shortcuts—if you type two spaces, the iPad inserts a period, adds a single space after, and automatically capitalizes the next letter. This is a quick and easy shortcut for starting new sentences, but you can turn it off.

- **Software Keyboard Layouts:** Somewhat "hidden" in the international keyboard settings, you can change between options such as the standard QWERTY layout and alternatives, the AZERTY and QWERTZ layouts. (These alternative layouts are said to allow for faster typing and lower odds of injury.)

- **Hardware Keyboard Layouts:** To use a distinctive hardware keyboard with your iPad, you can choose from among United States, Dvorak, U.S. International/PC, U.S. Extended, and British and other language-related options.

Along with these specific settings, your iPad also enables you to stack up several "live" keyboards for various languages and then switch easily among them.

One of the interesting things about the iPad is that it's actually one of the easiest ways around to work with the various character sets for different languages, especially if you need to mix and match different keyboards. Using different physical and/or virtual keyboards on a personal computer can be a pain, and the system can get confused about what characters should be generated at any given time. The iPad makes it easy.

The iPad, at this writing, supports 54 keyboards, with eight varieties of Chinese, three of French, and so on. If you've ever struggled with multiple character sets, you might find the iPad a dream come true.

You can add a bunch of keyboards and switch among them easily. The iPad never gets confused about what characters should show up when you tap a key. It's fun and easy.

The iPad also has settings for each different type of keyboard—again, with lots of options and a great deal of flexibility.

This section explains how to change the settings for a keyboard, using the U.S. English-language QWERTY keyboard as an example. It also demonstrates how to add additional keyboards that you can then easily switch among. The steps are similar for whichever keyboard(s) you choose.

Follow these steps to change keyboard settings.

 LET ME TRY IT

Changing Keyboard Settings

1. From the Home screen, tap Settings; then tap General.

2. Tap Keyboard. Keyboard options appear, as shown in Figure 18.13.

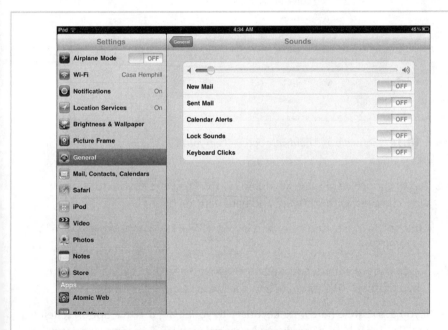

Figure 18.13 *The iPad gives you lots of keyboard control.*

3. Drag the sliders to turn typing-related features on and off, such as auto-capitalization, auto-correction, spell check, caps lock, and the end of sentence shortcut.

4. To change additional settings for your current keyboard or to add international keyboards, tap the International Keyboards button.

5. To change options for your default keyboard, tap the applicable button—in the United States and many other countries, the button is labeled English. Software and hardware options appear, as shown in Figure 18.14.

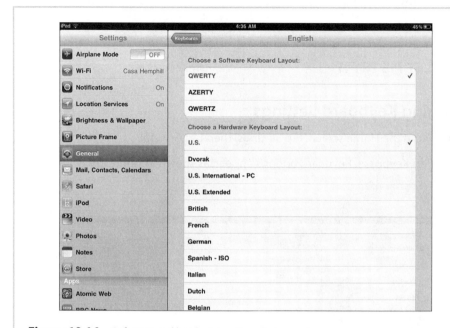

Figure 18.14   *Software and hardware options help you do even more.*

6. Tap to choose a software keyboard layout. Press the Keyboards button when finished with software and hardware keyboard layouts.

    Choose the most-used keyboard layout, QWERTY, or alternatives AZERTY or QWERTZ.

7. Tap to choose a hardware keyboard layout. Press the Keyboards button when finished with software and hardware keyboard layouts.

    If you associate a hardware keyboard to your iPad, use this option to tell the iPad what kind of hardware keyboard you use. Supported options should work well with the iPad.

8. To add a keyboard, tap Add New Keyboard. New keyboards appear, as shown in Figure 18.15.

    Any keyboards you add are available at a button-press when you enter text with your iPad.

9. Tap the keyboard you want to add. The keyboard is added to your list of available keyboards.

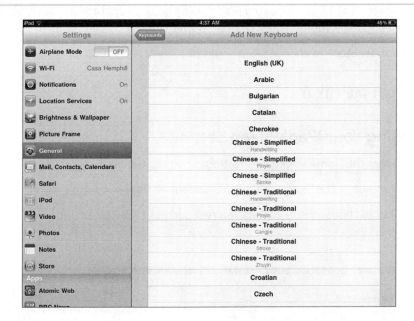

Figure 18.15 *Your iPad gives you lots of international options.*

10. To configure the keyboard, tap it to see the available options. Choose the Software Keyboard Layout and Hardware Keyboard Layout, repeating steps 5 through 7 for the new keyboard. The options for the additional keyboard are set.

11. To remove or re-order keyboards, press Edit. The edit screen appears.

12. To delete a keyboard from the list, tap the minus (–) key; then tap Delete to confirm. To re-order keyboards, drag the Towers of Hanoi icon on the right up and down. The keyboard list changes.

13. When finished, tap Done. Deleted keyboards are removed, and keyboards are re-ordered as specified.

Sleep Setting

Your iPad uses only a minimal amount of power when in sleep mode. You can put your iPad into sleep mode at any time by pressing the Sleep/Wake button.

Your iPad can also be set to go to sleep automatically after a certain period of time. I recommend that you set it to go to sleep after 15 minutes, the maximum amount of time you can choose without turning auto-lock off entirely.

With a setting of 15 minutes, your iPad doesn't go to sleep "too fast," but it doesn't stay on endlessly, running down battery power when you're not using it.

Follow these steps to change sleep settings.

 LET ME TRY IT

Changing Your iPad's Sleep Setting

1. From the Home screen, tap Settings; then tap General.

2. Tap Auto-Lock. Auto-Lock options appear, as shown in Figure 18.16.

3. Tap to choose the Auto-Lock interval, such as 15 minutes.

Figure 18.16 *It's easier to control your iPad's sleep than your own!*

index